by
S.K. Crocker

PublishAmerica
Baltimore

First printing

At the specific preference of the author, PublishAmerica allowed this work to remain exactly as the author intended, verbatim, without editorial input.

ISBN: 1-4241-3151-0
PUBLISHED BY PUBLISHAMERICA, LLLP
www.publishamerica.com
Baltimore

Printed in the United States of America

To Eric
Without you nothing would have been accomplished

Foreword

"Moreover thou shalt provide out of all the people able men, such as fear God, men of truth, hating covetousness; and place such over them, to be rulers of thousands, and rulers of hundreds, rulers of fifties, and rulers of tens": Exodus 18:21.

So you have become a Christian, a follower of Jesus Christ. Christ's apprentice so to speak.

Good for you. Welcome aboard. This is a decision, (just who's decision we'll discuss later), that will affect you for eternity and I know we'll meet when this earthly toil is finished. We are all here performing an important, albeit, temporary duty. We don't belong here but we are here, none the less. Just to make sure you understand what this means and what to expect, I'll tell you right now the world will hate you because they hated Jesus Christ before you. They were expecting a king. What they got was a Saviour.

So just what shall I do now, you ask. You have realized that Jesus was God sent to earth to make the supreme sacrifice. To me this is so logical for one of the main rules, here on earth, is that something has to die for something else to live. He overcame death and the grave. Jesus gave us this gift willingly because "the wages of sin is death" and no one has not sinned. No not one. Well, there's a war going on and like it or not you're part of it. This war is about people's souls. The war is about changing the world. This war is about freedom. This war is not easily won. It will require endurance and faith. It will require you to understand the importance of "listening" to God.

The government can't change the world no matter how many laws they make. In fact our government can't even understand it's own makeup let alone what constitutes spiritual warfare. It has come to the point, here in the new millennium, when the laws that government has made are in conflict with the word of God. You have to choose which ones you will comply with and which ones you will not. When Rome was falling, Octavius, a senator and legal scholar, made the following remark on the floor of the Roman senate, "There are two roads to anarchy. One when there is no law and two, when there is one law too many." In these latter days we find ourselves with more than one law too many. Laws meant to silence both Christians and the word of God. More on that later, for now, suffice it to say, we are clearly coming to a point in history when sides are being chosen. The spiritual warrior will have to decide which human law he will obey and which he will have to set aside. Render what is Caesar's unto Caesar only goes so far. Obeying government edicts is only right as long as the government pays attention to the commandments of God. I know what the "church" is saying about what I am writing. They are all reciting Romans 13 so I will explain,

1: Let every soul be subject unto the higher powers. For there is no power but of God: the powers that be are ordained of God.

2: Whosoever therefore resisteth the power, resisteth the ordinance of God: and they that resist shall receive to themselves damnation.

3: For rulers are not a terror to good works, but to the evil. Wilt thou then not be afraid of the power? do that which is good, and thou shalt have praise of the same:

4: For he is the minister of God to thee for good. But if thou do that which is evil, be afraid; for he beareth not the sword in vain: for he is the minister of God, a revenger to execute wrath upon him that doeth evil.

5: Wherefore ye must needs be subject, not only for wrath, but also for conscience sake.

6: For this cause pay ye tribute also: for they are God's ministers, attending continually upon this very thing.

7: Render therefore to all their dues: tribute to whom tribute is due; custom to whom custom; fear to whom fear; honour to whom honour. Romans 13:1-7

It is clear that Paul is telling the church that they are to respect their government. Here is the rub, NOT ALL GOVERNMENTS ARE TO BE RESPECTED! There is a danger, when reading the Bible, to take things out of context. Paul is actually stating the obvious that as long as the government is acting in good faith toward its subjects it is to be acknowledged as coming from God. But you cannot ignore the rest of the Word just on this part of Romans.

Look at Acts 12:21-23,

21: And upon a set day Herod, arrayed in royal apparel, sat upon his throne, and made an oration unto them.

22: And the people gave a shout, saying, It is the voice of a god, and not of a man.

23: And immediately the angel of the Lord smote him, because he gave not God the glory: and he was eaten of worms, and gave up the ghost.

Herod was the government. He had been after Paul to place him back in jail or to kill him. Here's what happened. When he refused to stop his persecution and agreed with the people that he was a god the Supreme Commander, through one of the angels, took him out.

While it is true that God ordains governments He expects them to give Him the glory and to use their power for the good of their people. What happens when governments no longer obey His will? He takes them out! Governments should never be looked upon as holy or divine. They are just institutions run by men, men, no different from you or me.

The government of the United States is in a different category. Our's was originally designed as a Republic and as such the people are the rulers. Romans 13 reads entirely different in this light. Verse one could read, Let every representative be subject to the higher power of the people.

Our battle manual(the Holy Bible) is filled with such stories of what happens when governments turn their back on God. He takes them out! The rulers are removed and God uses whatever tools He deems necessary to facilitate their removal.

God is the great I Am. He is completely clear and fine like a starlit night. God has inexhaustible power. He is the God that spoke and all of creation came into exsistance. God created all this for, only, His pleasure. Before the creation He elected all those that would spend eternity with Him. He is a God who is gentle with those that call on His name but He is also a God of war.

Many declare that the United States is a secular nation. In other words a nation not subject or bound to any religious rule. Do you realize what that means? Speaking for you, fellow warriors, these people are trying to take God out of our government. Let me tell you this recruit, THAT DECLARATION IS A LIE! When God is removed, by our people, there is a void and that void is being quickly filled by humanism.

Strictly speaking humanism is a system of thought that attaches prime importance to human rather than divine matters. An interesting sidelight to this is that during the Renaissance the humanistic movement was insidious. They tried to do away with the study of the Bible and scholarly books in favor of resurrecting the mythology of Greece and Rome. Their agenda was never realized. When the creation denies the Creator even the stones of the field will declare His holy name.

In the end humanists believe there is no God (see Psalms 14:1.) In a humanist church the people believe that God is at best inept and that He needs our help.

This religion of humanism believes, (and don't think for a moment it is not a religion) God is no longer sufficient. Peace and love are turned into war and hate. No longer are the people rejoicing in God's blessings but obeying a satanic cult that worships death and destruction. They deny that God never changes and strive to "save" themselves.

When humanism takes over, they require an unswerving loyalty from all the people. There are several keys to recognizing humanism and it's effect on the government. First the government naturally expands and its voice is heard to say, "If you don't agree with me you are not a loyal countryman." The church will be dragged in, paying homage by accepting a tax-free status, only to have it used against them. Men will try and perfect themselves through their own strategies like abortion, euthanasia and cloning.

Does any of this sound familiar? Religion cannot change the world no matter how many rules and dogmas they enact. Indeed, religion has partitioned itself into so many factions it is difficult to stick to many of their rules without violating the word of God. Jesus told us that the only way to change the world was to change the hearts of others…One at a time.

Individuals are the key. What is good for the few is good for the many. This is the catch phrase of the Kingdom of God. Think of the individuals that Jesus worked with. The men and women that He took a personal interest in. He knew them, what was in their heart and how they would react to His message.

You, fellow Christian, have chosen a side in this war. It won't be easy. You are just as susceptible to the enemy's slings and arrows as anyone. Without being properly equipped for this war, you will be ineffective. Without the basics you will be run over by the enemy and find yourself retreating constantly. Retreat, in and of itself, is not a bad thing as long as the time is used to muster up the fortitude and training needed to get back in the battle. Both fortitude and training can be found in our battle manual, The Holy Bible.

The first rule of the battle is to remember, scripture says that Satan comes ONLY to steal, kill and destroy. The devil is the enemy. Even such a luminary as Paul was buffeted by the enemy,

And lest I should be exalted above measure through the abundance of the revelations, there was given to me a thorn in the flesh, the messenger of Satan to buffet me, lest I should be exalted above measure. 2 Cor.12: 7.

You will be too. As I have said, before, you won't get a whole lot of help from the institutions. The churches have their own agenda and if you find a way to fit in you may find help. That's not to say that you are to disdain other believers but you need to find those that are in the thick of the battle. Not those that sit on the side lines. Too many of our churches, these days, are of the variety that precludes any meaningful discussion. Their "call to worship" means sit down, shut up and listen. This is not what you need as a warrior. By all means go out and find those fellow believers who are on the front lines. They are your support and indispensable to your personal struggle. These believers will help you stay the course. They will be your comfort in times of trouble and doubt. The government, at best, will turn a blind eye to your struggle. Remember who controls the kingdoms of the world, (Matt. 4: 8&9). At worse they can't and won't understand and will actively fight against you. Remember all governments are collectives and your primary directive is to preach the Gospel(good news) to individuals…one at a time.

The idea for this book was inspired by the vast number of "Call to Battle" books that have flooded the market recently. While a call to battle is needed and well-founded, it occurred to me that little if any thing was being said of just how this battle would be fought, i.e., the logistics and tactics that could and would be used on this battlefield.

I, personally, have been engaged in this battle for forty-five years and have learned a lot. Praise God! Not to say that I have learned it all but the one thing I have learned is that NO GOOD DEED GOES UNPUNISHED! The devil and his cohorts do not take the battle lightly and neither can you. There is an old saying that, "All's fair in love and war" and this adage is particularly true of spiritual warfare. Once you have enlisted in this battle the devil and his minions will bring all their considerable power against you. I would be derelict in my own duty if I didn't warn you just what to expect: Persecution (both demonic and religious), rejection, insult, slander, discreditation, betrayal, false accusation, hatred (religious and racial), ridicule, temptation and the suffering that come from resistance.

8: Be sober, be vigilant; because your adversary the devil, as a roaring lion, walketh about, seeking whom he may devour:

9: Whom resist stedfast in the faith, knowing that the same afflictions are accomplished in your brethren that are in the world.

10: But the God of all grace, who hath called us unto his eternal glory by Christ Jesus, after that ye have suffered a while, make you perfect, stablish, strengthen, settle you. 1 Pet. 5:8-10.

In other words if you are going to be part of this spiritual warfare there is going to be an element of suffering while you are under attack by the enemy. Remember, though, WE are going to be prepared. God doesn't need any crash test dummies in this war. He needs trained individuals who are aware of what is going to happen and are ready with their defenses. This book will help to see that you are properly equipped and trained. We will explore how to use our weapons, how to obey the Supreme Commander and we will learn to understand His battle plan.

Do not fear for, "Greater is He that is in you than he that is in the world," Paul wrote,

3: For though we walk in the flesh, we do not war after the flesh:

4: (For the weapons of our warfare are not carnal, but mighty through God to the pulling down of strong holds;)

5: Casting down imaginations, and every high thing that exalteth itself against the knowledge of God, and bringing into captivity every thought to the obedience of Christ; 2 Cor. 10 3-5.

Now I'll let you in on a little secret, WE WIN! Together we are going to explore the battle plan. Together we are going to go through basic training where we will explore the weapons we will be using and how to exercise for the best effect. In Advanced Training we will study logistics and tactics. All the various technics that will be explored will be explained using our battle manual, the Holy Bible, so let's get started. The battle is raging in the street. Reinforcements are vitally needed on all fronts. As the apostle Paul wrote to Timothy so very long ago,

This charge I commit unto thee, son Timothy, according to the prophesies which went before on thee, that thou by them mightest wage a good warfare ; 1 Tim. 1:18. .

BASIC TRAINING
Part One

Just What is a Christian?

Pretty simple question, huh? I decided to look up the word, "Christian" here's what my thesaurus says:

[n.] a religious person who believes in Jesus Christ and is a member of a Christian denomination.

[adj.] following the teachings or manifesting the qualities or spirit of Jesus Christ.

Let's start with the noun classification. First we'll break it down. Remember these definitions are written by someone who may or may not be a Christian.

A religious person. Whoa, hold on there, my Jesus had very little good to say about the religious people in His time so let's throw out that classification right away.

Who believes in Jesus Christ. Well I should hope so but does that go far enough? You see, fellow believers, Jesus doesn't just want us to believe in Him even the devil and his demons believe in Him. In reality it is simple what Jesus wants from you…EVERYTHING. He wants your heart. He wants your soul. He wants your body. The Supreme Commander wants your mind. He longs to be in a personal relationship with you. God wants you to open yourself so that He can be allowed to work through you. Jesus wants to be the Supreme

Commander. I'll take that further, He is the Supreme Commander it is just up to us to wake up and realize that fact.

President John F. Kennedy once proclaimed, "Ask not what your country can do for you but ask what you can do for your country." Jesus proclaims, "Ask not what you can do for God but what your God can do through you." Whatever happens don't let yourself get to a point where you are saying, What can I do for God today? The answer is nothing! He owns the cattle on a thousand hills. He created the universe. The earth and all of its inhabitants were created for Him. There is nothing that you can do for Him and it is only our arrogance and the tempting of the devil that makes us believe that we can. The only thing we can do is open ourselves to the indwelling of His Holy Spirit so that He can use us in the way that He has planned to change the minds and hearts of people.

Once out into the battle fields your chances of survival, relying on what you can do will amount to about the same as that proverbial ice cube in you know where. We haven't the mind, the skill or the aptitude to fight the devil on equal grounds. Only with the Supreme Commander guiding us and working through us do we stand a chance. Once the battle starts the devil will pull every dirty trick that he ever devised. He will attack your mind he will attack your soul and he will attack your body. Satan will attack your friends and he will attack your family. He will take the good that you do and make it seem as if it's evil. The institutions, be they governments or religions, will fight against you. He will attack your finances. The devil has more tricks than we can imagine and he'll use everyone to take you out of the fight. Did I mention that WE WIN!

The next phrase reads, is a member of a Christian denomination. A poll I read just a few days ago said that almost 80% of United States citizens referred to themselves as Christian. That same poll stated that only 30% attended a church regularly. That leaves a lot of confessed Christians out of the definition. We'll elaborate about that later.

So that brings us to the adjective definition: following the teachings or manifesting the qualities or spirit of Jesus Christ. There you go. I personally prefer being called a follower of Jesus Christ than a Christian. Maybe it's the negative connotation of the down right terrible things done by people claiming to be Christians or maybe just the "religious" connotations, I don't know, but this I do know, the church is not a building it is people and it is my daily prayer that I might manifest the qualities of my Master. We will study more on just what the qualities of the Supreme Commander are but for now, be an adjective. Not a noun.

Election

Election, simply, means something or someone who is "picked out." In the case of this study it refers to the question of who does the picking. Do we choose to be a Christian or are we chosen as a Christian? Who decides on our course of action? I am not interested in religious dogma and rules what interests me is what my Bible has to say. So here goes. Bear with me.

32: And before him shall be gathered all nations: and he shall separate them one from another, as a shepherd divideth his sheep from the goats:

33: And he shall set the sheep on his right hand, but the goats on the left.

34: Then shall the King say unto them on his right hand, Come, ye blessed of my Father, inherit the kingdom prepared for you from the foundation of the world: Matt. 25:32-34.

Father, I will that they also, whom thou hast given me, be with me where I am; that they may behold my glory, which thou hast given me: for thou lovedst me before the foundation of the world. John 17:24.

4: According as he hath chosen us in him before the foundation of the world, that we should be holy and without blame before him in love:

5: Having predestinated us unto the adoption of children by Jesus Christ to himself, according to the good pleasure of his will, Eph. 1: 4&5.

God has known us from the foundations of the earth, before we were knit in the womb. (John 17:24) Since the beginning of time God has known of us and has chosen us. Jesus makes it plain in John 15: 16&19.

16: Ye have not chosen me, but I have chosen you, and ordained you, that ye should go and bring forth fruit, and that your fruit should remain: that at all ye shall ask of the Father in my name, he may give it you.

19: If ye were of the world, the world would love his own: but because ye are not of the world, but I have chosen you out of the world, therefore the world hateth you.

God has predestined who we are. Eph. 1:4&5.

4: According as he hath chosen us in him before the foundation of the world, that we should be holy and without blame before him in love:

5: Having predestinated us unto the adoption of children by Jesus Christ to himself, according to the good pleasure of his will,

That word predestinated is an interesting word. In the Greek it means having decided since eternity. In the English it refers to destiny. The desire of God to choose someone for a particular fate or purpose. In a later chapter we'll explore those desires that God has for His people. What jobs we are to fulfill and how we will fulfill them, for now, remember the prime directive; You cannot "do" for God. You must let Him do through you.

We are the elect of God. He chose us for the work in front of us. The apostles were well aware of this. 1 Peter 1:2.

2: Elect according to the foreknowledge of God the Father, through sanctification of the Spirit, unto obedience and sprinkling of the blood of Jesus Christ: Grace unto you, and peace, be multiplied.

4: Knowing, brethren beloved, your election of God. 1 Thes 1:4.

If we are all elected to God's salvation why do we need to preach the gospel? Why, if all Christians are predestined to believe, is the gospel commanded to be preached? We could say, as spiritual warriors, simply because the Supreme Commander commands it but there is more to the "good news" than that.

16: For I am not ashamed of the gospel of Christ: for it is the power of God unto salvation to every one that believeth; to the Jew first, and also to the Greek.

17: For therein is the righteousness of God revealed from faith to faith: as it is written, The just shall live by faith. Romans 1:16&17.

The gospel is the power of God. His righteousness is revealed through His gospel.

15: And how shall they preach, except they be sent? as it is written, How beautiful are the feet of them that preach the gospel of peace, and bring glad tidings of good things!

16: But they have not all obeyed the gospel. For Esaias saith, Lord, who hath believed our report?

17: So then faith cometh by hearing, and hearing by the word of God. Romans 10: 15&16.

Our faith is built upon the gospel. The good news that is the word of God. Finally there is a blessing for those that spread that good news,

And I am sure that, when I come unto you, I shall come in the fullness of the blessing of the gospel of Christ. Romans 15:29.

It is imperative that the gospel be preached for the elect's sake. We are the ones in the battle. Whose very lives are at stake.

I recall a time when I ran for public office. It was a hard battle. The forces of humanism were fighting to rule and anyone in

19

disagreement with them was setting themselves up for ridicule. Late one night I received a phone call and having answered, the conversation went something like this,

"Are you that Christian guy whose running for election?"

"Yes sir, I am."

"I just wanted to tell you that we don't appreciate your opinions. I suggest that you drop out now before something bad happens to you or someone in your family."

The phone went dead. I stood for a long time just looking at the useless receiver cradled in my hand. Granted my first emotion was fear. Then the fear turned to anger. Anger at myself, mostly, for putting my family in jeopardy. I think that it was the use of the caller's word election that jolted me out of my anger and the next words to enter my mind were,

"Father protect us." He always has and always will. Praise His holy name.

So it is now self evident that it is God who chooses us, not we who choose Him. So now what to do with this knowledge? Are we to merrily go about our life knowing that our eternity is secure and that there is no need to do anything? Heaven forbid. James told us that faith without works is dead. The thing that needs emphazing here is that we cannot "do" for God, He can only do for you and through you. It is my sincere belief that we, as followers of the risen Christ, are here on earth for a reason. We have a job to do. If we were foreordained to be here and to serve a risen Savior then logically there is a reason. So our first job is to find out that reason. In reality, I believe that all of you, who are reading this book, already have a suspicion on just what that reason is. For the others and to help us on this road of discovery our battle manual lists those reasons.

1: Now concerning spiritual gifts, brethren, I would not have you ignorant.

2: Ye know that ye were Gentiles, carried away unto these dumb idols, even as ye were led.

3: Wherefore I give you to understand, that no man speaking by the Spirit of God calleth Jesus accursed: and that no man can say that Jesus is the Lord, but by the Holy Ghost.

4: Now there are diversities of gifts, but the same Spirit.

5: And there are differences of administrations, but the same Lord.

6: And there are diversities of operations, but it is the same God which worketh all in all.

7: But the manifestation of the Spirit is given to every man to profit withal.

8: For to one is given by the Spirit the word of wisdom; to another the word of knowledge by the same Spirit;

9: To another faith by the same Spirit; to another the gifts of healing by the same Spirit;

10: To another the working of miracles; to another prophecy; to another discerning of spirits; to another divers kinds of tongues; to another the interpretation of tongues: 1 Cor. 12:1-10.

These are not singular gifts but some will have a combination of these gifts. Keep in mind that these gifts are not for our own edification but to promote God's Kingdom on earth.

Wisdom

Wisdom is based on a body of knowledge and experience of God.

12: But before all these, they shall lay their hands on you, and persecute you, delivering you up to the synagogues, and into prisons, being brought before kings and rulers for my name's sake.

13: And it shall turn to you for a testimony.

14: Settle it therefore in your hearts, not to meditate before what ye shall answer:

15: For I will give you a mouth and wisdom, which all your adversaries shall not be able to gainsay nor resist. Luke 21: 12-15.

There you have it. The gift of wisdom comes from God working through you. Wisdom is the act of knowing that even disasters can be used as a testimony for the Kingdom. There is a song in contemporary Christian music whose chorus begins, "I pledge allegiance to the Lamb, " what finer anthem could any spiritual warrior have? When the time comes (and I believe that it is right around the corner) the government and religion will begin to drag Christians before them as in the days of Rome. It doesn't take much imagination, these days, to equate the Roman soldiers with the "alphabet soup" agencies that make up our government's enforcement arm. As for the religious side the same applies, The World Council of Churches wields considerable power to punish those that go outside their rules and there is considerable danger in the tax exempt status of most denominations. What the government giveth the government can taketh away if certain rules are not adhered to.

Our Supreme Commander said very little when He was brought before the authorities. The conversation between Him and Pilate is very telling of how the spiritual warrior should react,

37: Pilate therefore said unto him, Art thou a king then? Jesus answered, Thou sayest that I am a king. To this end was I born, and for this cause came I into the world, that I should bear witness unto the truth. Every one that is of the truth heareth my voice.

38: Pilate saith unto him, What is truth? John 18:37&38.

What is truth? Mr. Pilate He had just told you what the truth is. Those without an ear will never hear, dear friends, to go on would have been useless.

The spiritual warrior is admonished in Proverbs 1:7,

The fear of the LORD is the beginning of knowledge: but fools despise wisdom and instruction.

Then we are told where wisdom comes from in 2:6,

For the LORD giveth wisdom: out of his mouth cometh knowledge and understanding.

Our battle manual holds the key to wisdom.

Get wisdom, get understanding: forget it not; neither decline from the words of my mouth. Proverbs 4:5.

Wisdom is easy to receive but difficult to hang on to. It requires "remembering."

1: O God, thou art my God; early will I seek thee: my soul thirsteth for thee, my flesh longeth for thee in a dry and thirsty land, where no water is;

2: To see thy power and thy glory, so as I have seen thee in the sanctuary.

3: Because thy lovingkindness is better than life, my lips shall praise thee.

4: Thus will I bless thee while I live: I will lift up my hands in thy name.

5: My soul shall be satisfied as with marrow and fatness; and my mouth shall praise thee with joyful lips:

6: When I remember thee upon my bed, and meditate on thee in the night watches.

7: Because thou hast been my help, therefore in the shadow of thy wings will I rejoice.

8: My soul followeth hard after thee: thy right hand upholdeth me. Psalms 63:1-8.

Pay close attention to verse three."Thy lovingkindness is better than life." The men of the Bible meant what they said. By today's standards these were not educated men but they had the inspiration of Almighty God to teach them. The Lord's truth and love are better than being alive. What a statement. What a blessing. No King but Jesus.

Knowledge

Knowledge is information and skills acquired through experience or education.

1: Simon Peter, a servant and an apostle of Jesus Christ, to them that have obtained like precious faith with us through the righteousness of God and our Saviour Jesus Christ:

2: Grace and peace be multiplied unto you through the knowledge of God, and of Jesus our Lord,

3: According as his divine power hath given unto us all things that pertain unto life and godliness, through the knowledge of him that hath called us to glory and virtue:

4: Whereby are given unto us exceeding great and precious promises: that by these ye might be partakers of the divine nature, having escaped the corruption that is in the world through lust.

5: And beside this, giving all diligence, add to your faith virtue; and to virtue knowledge;

6: And to knowledge temperance; and to temperance patience; and to patience godliness;

7: And to godliness brotherly kindness; and to brotherly kindness charity.

8: For if these things be in you, and abound, they make you that ye shall neither be barren nor unfruitful in the knowledge of our Lord Jesus Christ. 1 Peter 1:1-8.

The gift of knowledge comes from God working through you. Virtue is simply behavior that shows a high moral standard. More on that later but for now suffice it to say virtue rates high in the order of these gifts. Peter makes reference here that through the Supreme Commander's divine power(also, more on that later) we have knowledge that pertains to life and godliness. When the Christian can make that leap from worldly knowledge of life to the true knowledge of life, he can then call himself a spiritual warrior. With study, prayer and faith he, then, can begin to understand the will of God.

Faith

Faith means to have complete trust and confidence in Almighty God. Along with Grace these are two concepts that must be addressed at length.

5: That your faith should not stand in the wisdom of men, but in the power of God. 1 Cor. 2:5

The gift of faith is in the power of God. Through the Holy Spirit God wants us to be totally dependant on Him. We will explore this "faith," in depth, in a later chapter.

Healing

Healing means to make sound or put right.

38: How God anointed Jesus of Nazareth with the Holy Ghost and with power: who went about doing good, and healing all that were oppressed of the devil; for God was with him. Acts 10:38.

The gift of healing requires that God be with you. The true intention of the gift of healing is showing God's love to the world and to relieve the oppression brought on by the enemy.

Healing can take on different dimensions than just the healing of the body. Our minds can also be healed as well as the soul. The enemy delights in obstructing our minds with feelings of inadequacy and doubt. Remember who you are. God can heal the mind. When the mind and body are in need of healing the soul will be affected as well. A broken heart is really the soul's illness. God mends broken hearts and replaces the illness with new found hope and faith in Him.

It is quite easy for Satan to misdirect the spiritual warrior with the cares of this world. He makes what we would normally find repulsive, alluring with his lies. Take care that you are protected by God. We cannot do it by ourselves. Relying on self equals failure. In a spiritual warrior resides the most powerful force in the universe, the

Holy Ghost. Use Him. Depend on Him. Keep your feet on the battle field but your mind and soul must live on the promises of God. His lovingkindness IS better than life.

Miracles

Miracles are welcomed events that are extraordinary.

22: Ye men of Israel, hear these words; Jesus of Nazareth, a man approved of God among you by miracles and wonders and signs, which God did by him in the midst of you, as ye yourselves also know: Acts 2:22

The gift of miracles needs approval from God and to Him be the glory. We are vessels, the true worker of miracles is God. But there is something else that needs to be noted,

12: Verily, verily, I say unto you, He that believeth on me, the works that I do shall he do also; and greater works than these shall he do; because I go unto my Father.

13: And whatsoever ye shall ask in my name, that will I do, that the Father may be glorified in the Son. John 14: 12&13.

I say it again these men were inspired by God and God is not a man that He should lie. We are to do, through our faith, greater miracles than even the Supreme Commander.

I have had the blessing of seeing many miracles performed by the Supreme Commander and at each occurrence one could feel the presence of Almighty God. One that clearly comes to mind was while I was studying pre-med in the 1970's at a small college in the Pacific Northwest. We were being shown a film on the birth of a human child. This film was shot at 400 frames per second, under an electron microscope, to slow the process of the cells of an embryo dividing at the moment of conception. Mind you this was being filmed at the highest possible speed so that the student might see the actual division. The actual division was like a spark. It appeared in the blinking of an eye. The slowing process could not capture that moment when God, Himself, touched the cells and instead of one there were two. Praise His mighty name.

Prophesy

Prophesy is the ability to predict by writing or the spoken word usually by divine inspiration.

3: And I will give power unto my two witnesses, and they shall prophesy a thousand two hundred and threescore days, clothed in sackcloth. Rev. 11:3.

The gift of prophesy requires the power of God. Are you getting the drift of this message yet?

Prophesy can be for or against, (see Ezekiel). It can be a warning or a promise. It can foretell future events but one thing to be certain of is that if it is true prophesy it will be the Supreme Commander speaking through man and not of their own deviations. There are prophets of God and prophets of Satan. Be sure to test the prophets before heeding their proclamations.

1: Follow after charity, and desire spiritual gifts, but rather that ye may prophesy.

2: For he that speaketh in an unknown tongue speaketh not unto men, but unto God: for no man understandeth him; howbeit in the spirit he speaketh mysteries.

3: But he that prophesieth speaketh unto men to edification, and exhortation, and comfort.

Here are some ways to test those prophets and their prophesies. Are they meant to instruct or improve, morally, the Body of Christ? Are they meant to strongly encourage or urge the warrior to act? Do the prophesies relay a sense of ease? Do they free someone from pain? Are the prophesies meant to free the oppressed? Console those that mourn or are worried? The old Latin word that comfort is derived from means to strengthen. Test the prophesies. Do they strengthen the spiritual warrior?

Having then gifts differing according to the grace that is given to us, whether prophecy, let us prophesy according to the proportion of faith; Romans 12:6.

Paul is alluding to an ability to judge the relative importance of things when he uses the word proportion. Also, he refers to a relationship with the whole body of knowledge. Make sure what the prophesy is saying makes sense.

One of the great prophesies that I have heard was when former President Gerald Ford, standing in the White House rose garden said, "America is in deep trouble." President Ford probably had no idea that he was being a prophet but the prophesy itself stands discernment. It freed a lot of people who were oppressed by the lies of Satan.

As we enter the battle field, in these latter days, don't forget what Joel wrote. It is more revelent today than any other time in the history of man on this planet,

And it shall come to pass afterward, that I will pour out my spirit upon all flesh; and your sons and your daughters shall prophesy, your old men shall dream dreams, your young men shall see visions: Joel 2:28.

Discerning of Spirits

Discerning of spirits means having the ability to show good judgement about the true meaning or intention of them opposed to a strict verbal interpretation.

1: And when he had called unto him his twelve disciples, he gave them power against unclean spirits, to cast them out, and to heal all manner of sickness and all manner of disease. Matt 10:1.

The gift is given through the power of Jesus Christ. We need to "separate", with all our senses, the spirits and their intentions. Intention is a valuable commodity. Is the aim of the spirits for the good of the warrior? Is the spirit's plan to the betterment of the Body of Christ? These questions need to be looked at with great care. Is the anticipation of results for the spiritual freedom of the warrior or for something else?

To get a handle on the discerning of spirits I suggest that you take the time to read 1 Timothy chapter four.

For God hath not given us the spirit of fear; but of power, and of love, and of a sound mind
2 Tim. 1:7.

There is an old saying that anger is a more useful emotion than fear. This is true in that fear is caused by the threat of danger, pain or harm. The likelihood of something un-toward happening to us. Anger, on the other hand, is the strong feeling of annoyance, displeasure or hostility. The root of anger comes from the Old Norse word meaning "grief." God, on the other hand, gives us power, love and understanding. Power to defeat the evil one. Love to make us aware of the fallibility of every one of us and the understanding that not all is as it seems to our mind.

Say to them that are of a fearful heart, Be strong, fear not: behold, your God will come with vengeance, even God with a recompence; he will come and save you. Isa. 35:4.

Tongues

This gift, I believe, has two meanings. Certainly the power of speaking in unknown languages is as alive in these latter days as it was in the days of the apostles. I have been a witness to the gift many times but I also believe that the gift of tongues is that ability that some have to express their feelings and opinions openly and logically.

4: And they were all filled with the Holy Ghost, and began to speak with other tongues, as the Spirit gave them utterance. Acts 2:4.

The gift, if tongues, is by the inspiration of the Holy Spirit wether, it is unknown tongues or a well-thought out book or oratory.

Interpretation of Tongues

If the gift is unknown tongues, they need to be interpreted.

5: I would that ye all spake with tongues, but rather that ye prophesied: for greater is he that prophesieth than he that speaketh with tongues, except he interprets, that the church may receive edifying. 1 Cor. 14:5.

In other words, what good would it be if no one understood the message brought by the unknown tongues?

I think my point is made. Whatever gift one has been given to do the job of spiritual warfare it must come from Almighty God. It is His gift made for His elect to function against the enemy and no I don't think it is any great mystery but a natural extension to our work here on earth. I believe that each one of you who reads this book knows exactly what gifts you have been given. I believe that the Holy Spirit has impressed on each warrior's heart just what it is that He would have them do. Now it is up to you as to wether you will obey or lock up those gifts. It is time for choosing sides.

A Word About Ephesians 4:11

And he gave some, apostles; and some, prophets; and some, evangelists; and some, pastors and teachers; As opposed to gifts these are the jobs that as a Christian you will be called upon to perform.

Apostles

Being an apostle simply means you are a messenger. An enthusiastic and pioneering supporter of the cause.

The message is the gospel. The cause is the cause of the Supreme Commander. (Read 2 Peter).

There are a number of suggestions on how the gospel should be preached in 1 Thes. Chapter 2.

Who are called to be apostles?

4: And declared to be the Son of God with power, according to the spirit of holiness, by the resurrection from the dead:

5: By whom we have received grace and apostleship, for obedience to the faith among all nations, for his name:

6: Among whom are ye also the called of Jesus Christ:

Sounds like all of us, huh recruit? What can we expect as we do the work of an apostle?

9: For I think that God hath set forth us the apostles last, as it were appointed to death: for we are made a spectacle unto the world, and to angels, and to men.

10: We are fools for Christ's sake, but ye are wise in Christ; we are weak, but ye are strong; ye are honourable, but we are despised.

11: Even unto this present hour we both hunger, and thirst, and are naked, and are buffeted, and have no certain dwellingplace; 1 Cor 4:9-11.

And laid their hands on the apostles, and put them in the common prison. Acts 5:8.

Told you it wouldn't be easy. Would you be a fool for Christ? There is an old saying, "fools rush in where angels fear to tread." Will you appear to be a person who lacks good judgement. That's the way the world looks at us. You know? Would you be weak so that Christ could be strong through you? Are you willing to be hated? In the end are you willing to go hungry? Thirsty? Naked? Attacked? Could you go on without a regular home? Will you risk prison for your God? These are all things that the spiritual warrior must be willing to endure for the sake of the Supreme Commander. Did I mention? WE WIN!

Prophets

A prophet is a person who teaches and proclaims the will of God. He can also be a person who predicts the future or advocates a new belief or theory. Remember the proverb, "There is nothing new under the sun."

Who are called to be prophets?

And Moses said unto him, Enviest thou for my sake? would God that all the LORD's people were prophets, and that the LORD would put his spirit upon them! Num. 11:29.

What to expect as a prophet?

Take, my brethren, the prophets, who have spoken in the name of the Lord, for an example of suffering affliction, and of patience. James 5:10.

WE WIN!

In addition to the Supreme Commander's prophets there are also false prophets.

Beloved, believe not every spirit, but try the spirits whether they

are of God: because many false prophets are gone out into the world.
1 John 4:1

But there were false prophets also among the people, even as there shall be false teachers among you, who privily shall bring in damnable heresies, even denying the Lord that bought them, and bring upon themselves swift destruction. 2 Peter 2:1.

Here's how to tell a false prophet,

Hereby know ye the Spirit of God: Every spirit that confesseth that Jesus Christ is come in the flesh is of God: 1 John 4:2.

Here's what will happen with these "treacherous" prophets and the cities and countries that they inhabit,

1: Woe to her that is filthy and polluted, to the oppressing city!

2: She obeyed not the voice; she received not correction; she trusted not in the LORD; she drew not near to her God.

3: Her princes within her are roaring lions; her judges are evening wolves; they gnaw not the bones till the morrow.

4: Her prophets are light and treacherous persons: her priests have polluted the sanctuary, they have done violence to the law.

5: The just LORD is in the midst thereof; he will not do iniquity: every morning doth he bring his judgment to light, he faileth not; but the unjust knoweth no shame.

6: I have cut off the nations: their towers are desolate; I made their streets waste, that none passeth by: their cities are destroyed, so that there is no man, that there is none inhabitant. Zeph. 3:1-6.

Spiritual warriors...Have you any ideas on just whom Zephaniah was speaking about? Read the entire third chapter of Zephaniah. Compare it to these latter days. I believe that this is his prophesy for our times. Pay special attention to the thirteenth verse.

As an old friend is known to say, "I am not a prophet nor do I play one on T.V. but I can read the word of God."

Evangelist

Someone who practices evangelism is a person who is a

passionate advocate of the word of God. One who seeks to convert others to the faith.

2: Preach the word; be instant in season, out of season; reprove, rebuke, exhort with all longsuffering and doctrine.

3: For the time will come when they will not endure sound doctrine; but after their own lusts shall they heap to themselves teachers, having itching ears;

4: And they shall turn away their ears from the truth, and shall be turned unto fables.

5: But watch thou in all things, endure afflictions, do the work of an evangelist, make full proof of thy ministry. 2 Tim 4: 2-5.

Itching ears. What a beautiful analogy. Ears that are willing to hear other doctrines or other gospels and actually go out of their way to find them. Seek ye first the Kingdom of God.

Timothy always makes his marching orders abundantly clear and always reminds us of the promises of God,

6: For I am now ready to be offered, and the time of my departure is at hand.

7: I have fought a good fight, I have finished my course, I have kept the faith:

8: Henceforth there is laid up for me a crown of righteousness, which the Lord, the righteous judge, shall give me at that day: and not to me only, but unto all them also that love his appearing. 2 Tim. 4:6-8.

Pastor

Pastor comes from the Latin word for "shepherd." He, or she, is responsible for leading a church or congregation.

And I will give you pastors according to mine heart, which shall feed you with knowledge and understanding. Jer. 3:15.

These are the jobs of a pastor. " Feed my sheep." Is what the

Supreme Commander told Peter. This is such an important job that dereliction of duty brings swift and terrible judgement,

1: Woe be unto the pastors that destroy and scatter the sheep of my pasture! saith the LORD. *2:* Therefore thus saith the LORD God of Israel against the pastors that feed my people; Ye have scattered my flock, and driven them away, and have not visited them: behold, I will visit upon you the evil of your doings, saith the LORD. Jer. 23:1&2.

Remember pastors, the job you do is for the benefit of individuals. Not for some council or committee. Unite and never scatter those you have been charged with. Feed those individuals with the word of God and not the words of men. Visit those individuals who have left. There are many reasons for leaving a congregation. Those spiritual warriors who have left still need you. Don't abandon them.

Teachers

A teacher is someone who relays the word of God to others and "teaches" them how to study and learn for themselves with the aid of the Holy Spirit.

It is important to remember that these gifts are not singular and can be found in combination in every spiritual warrior. It is, in my experience, that one of the gifts will stand out above the rest as a main gift.

Since the beginning of the gospel there have been false teachers. (We cover a few in this book but there are many others). Fortunately they don't have a long life expectancy.

But there were false prophets also among the people, even as there shall be false teachers among you, who privily shall bring in damnable heresies, even denying the Lord that bought them, and bring upon themselves swift destruction. 2 Peter 2:1.

35

It is important that teachers' remember that there are teachings for the "young in Christ" and the mature spiritual warrior.

12: For when for the time ye ought to be teachers, ye have need that one teach you again which be the first principles of the oracles of God; and are become such as have need of milk, and not of strong meat.

13: For every one that useth milk is unskillful in the word of righteousness: for he is a babe.

14: But strong meat belongeth to them that are of full age, even those who by reason of use have their senses exercised to discern both good and evil. Heb. 5:12-14.

Teachers can only accomplish a certain amount then it is up to us through the Holy Spirit,

98: Thou through thy commandments hast made me wiser than mine enemies: for they are ever with me.

99: I have more understanding than all my teachers: for thy testimonies are my meditation.

100: I understand more than the ancients, because I keep thy precepts. Psalms 119: 98-100.

Just who you are as a Christian

Now for some good news as a Christian you have become a new creature and as a new creature you have some new names. Here they are.

Saint

My dictionary defines a saint as a person who is acknowledged as holy or virtuous and regarded in Christian faith as in heaven after death. The word saint is taken from the Latin word sanctus which means "holy." Fellow believer you are a saint.

Unto the church of God which is at Corinth, to them that are sanctified in Christ Jesus, called to be saints, with all that in every place call upon the name of Jesus Christ our Lord, both theirs and ours: 1 Cor. 1:2

Do ye not know that the saints shall judge the world? and if the world shall be judged by you, are ye unworthy to judge the smallest matters? 1 Cor. 6:2.

26: Even the mystery which hath been hid from ages and from generations, but now is made manifest to his saints:

27: To whom God would make known what is the riches of the glory of this mystery among the Gentiles; which is Christ in you, the hope of glory:

28: Whom we preach, warning every man, and teaching every man in all wisdom; that we may present every man perfect in Christ Jesus: Col. 1:26-28.

Heirs of God

An heir is someone who is legally entitled to the property and rank of another and contributes to the work of a predecessor. Think about that when the enemy comes against you with feelings of inadequacy.

And if children, then heirs; heirs of God, and joint-heirs with Christ; if so be that we suffer with him, that we may be also glorified together. Rom. 8:17.

That being justified by his grace, we should be made heirs according to the hope of eternal life. Titus 3:7.

Just remember that it is your faith that furnishes you with these titles and not what you "do."

Child of God

You my dear saint are also a son of God. A child who knows his Father.

1: Behold, what manner of love the Father hath bestowed upon us, that we should be called the sons of God: therefore the world knoweth us not, because it knew him not.

2: Beloved, now are we the sons of God, and it doth not yet appear what we shall be: but we know that, when he shall appear, we shall be like him; for we shall see him as he is. 1 John 3 1&2.

For as many as are led by the Spirit of God, they are the sons of God. Rom. 8:14.

12: But as many as received him, to them gave he power to become the sons of God, even to them that believe on his name:

13: Which were born, not of blood, nor of the will of the flesh, nor of the will of man, but of God. John 12&13.

13: For it is God which worketh in you both to will and to do of his good pleasure.

14: Do all things without murmurings and disputings:

15: That ye may be blameless and harmless, the sons of God, without rebuke, in the midst of a crooked and perverse nation, among whom ye shine as lights in the world; Phil. 2:13-15.

Friends of God

Imagine that you have a new friend and this friend is the most powerful person in the universe. Imagine no more.

14: Ye are my friends, if ye do whatsoever I command you.

15: Henceforth I call you not servants; for the servant knoweth not what his lord doeth: but I have called you friends; for all things that I have heard of my Father I have made known unto you. John 15:14&15.

And I say unto you my friends, Be not afraid of them that kill the body, and after that have no more that they can do. Luke 12:4.

Over comers

Here's what our Supreme Commander said to His apostles,
These things I have spoken unto you, that in me ye might have peace. In the world ye shall have tribulation: but be of good cheer; I have overcome the world. John 16:33.

Here's what He says about us,

4: For whatsoever is born of God overcometh the world: and this is the victory that overcometh the world, even our faith.

5: Who is he that overcometh the world, but he that believeth that Jesus is the Son of God? 1 John 5:4&5.

What does it mean to be over comers? It means that WE WIN! Just like our Supreme Commander we have over come the world, death and the grave. Praise His holy name. Along with this gift he gives other promises for those of us over comers,

He that hath an ear, let him hear what the Spirit saith unto the churches; To him that overcometh will I give to eat of the tree of life, which is in the midst of the paradise of God. Rev. 2:7.

We will live forever with the Supreme Commander in heaven.

He that hath an ear, let him hear what the Spirit saith unto the churches; He that overcometh shall not be hurt of the second death. Rev. 2:11.

We will live forever in communion with the Creator of the Universe.

He that hath an ear, let him hear what the Spirit saith unto the churches; To him that overcometh will I give to eat of the hidden manna, and will give him a white stone, and in the stone a new name written, which no man knoweth saving he that receiveth it. Rev 2:17.

The marvelous thing about our God is that he never speaks in riddles and if He writes something that might be a little hard to understand He always explains it elsewhere. For instance,

To him that overcometh will I give to eat of the hidden manna, John 6:56-58.

56: He that eateth my flesh, and drinketh my blood, dwelleth in me, and I in him.

57: As the living Father hath sent me, and I live by the Father: so he that eateth me, even he shall live by me.

58: This is that bread which came down from heaven: not as your fathers did eat manna, and are dead: he that eateth of this bread shall live for ever and will give him a white stone. Isa. 28:16.

Therefore thus saith the Lord GOD, Behold, I lay in Zion for a foundation a stone, a tried stone, a precious corner stone, a sure foundation: he that believeth shall not make haste.

and in the stone a new name written. Rev. 3:12.

Him that overcometh will I make a pillar in the temple of my God, and he shall go no more out: and I will write upon him the name of my God, and the name of the city of my God, which is new Jerusalem, which cometh down out of heaven from my God: and I will write upon him my new name.

26: And he that overcometh, and keepeth my works unto the end, to him will I give power over the nations:

We will have power over the nations.

27: And he shall rule them with a rod of iron; as the vessels of a potter shall they be broken to shivers: even as I received of my Father.

28: And I will give him the morning star. Rev 2: 26-28.

Who is the morning star?

I Jesus have sent mine angel to testify unto you these things in the churches. I am the root and the offspring of David, and the bright and morning star. Rev. 22:16.

He that overcometh, the same shall be clothed in white raiment; and I will not blot out his name out of the book of life, but I will confess his name before my Father, and before his angels. Rev 3:5.

The Supreme Commander is our defense attorney.

To him that overcometh will I grant to sit with me in my throne, even as I also overcame, and am set down with my Father in his throne. Rev. 3:21

We will rule along with the Supreme Commander.
There are other names as well that we can claim through the word,
9: But ye are a chosen generation, a royal priesthood, an holy nation, a peculiar people; that ye should shew forth the praises of him who hath called you out of darkness into his marvelous light:
10: Which in time past were not a people, but are now the people of God: which had not obtained mercy, but now have obtained mercy.
11: Dearly beloved, I beseech you as strangers and pilgrims, abstain from fleshly lusts, which war against the soul; 1 Peter 2: 9-11.

A chosen generation, a generation of the elect. A set of members of a family, the Body of Christ, all bound together in a single stage of descent.
A royal priesthood. We have the status of the King as a member of His family. We are a member of the royal family. The elect are of

royal ancestry, princes of the royal blood. We belong to the Supreme Commander and are invested with royal power. As priests, ordained ministers of the Body of Christ, we are authorized to carry on His work.

A holy nation, dedicated to God and morally and spiritually excellent, through the Holy Spirit. We belong and are derived from Almighty God. We are to be associated with His divine power. We are a large body of people united by our common Master. Inhabiting the earth as born again followers of the Supreme Commander. We are a holy people under a single government. As warriors we are a people bound by a common heritage. As a people, we will one day occupy the land of our birth as conquerors.

A peculiar people. Strangers in a strange land where we don't belong. Belonging exclusively to the Lord God Almighty. In the direct jurisdiction of the Supreme Commander. We are private property. We are not of the familiar or customary, we are, " out of the ordinary." Ultimately we are the mass of the citizens of heaven.

We are strangers, not really known on this planet. We are pilgrims in our journey to heaven. Foreign to this world.

Lastly,

He that overcometh shall inherit all things; and I will be his God, and he shall be my son. Rev. 21:7.

Guess you can't do much better than inheriting EVERYTHING! Thank you, Father.

Faith and Grace

Faith

In Hebrews 11:1 Paul defines faith,

Now faith is the substance of things hoped for, the evidence of things not seen.

In other word's faith is complete trust and confidence in the Supreme Commander. A feeling of expectation that Jesus Christ will fill our every need as He said He would,

And Jesus said unto them, Because of your unbelief: for verily I say unto you, If ye have faith as a grain of mustard seed, ye shall say unto this mountain, Remove hence to yonder place; and it shall remove; and nothing shall be impossible unto you. Matt. 17:20.

Faith is the only way to please the Supreme Commander,

But without faith it is impossible to please him: for he that cometh to God must believe that he is, and that he is a rewarder of them that diligently seek him. Heb. 11:6.

Now the just shall live by faith: but if any man draw back, my soul shall have no pleasure in him. Heb. 10:38.

In other words those that would be morally right and fair, who would do those things that are appropriate or deserved are to live their lives by faith. We will look into this faith business more when we are ready to outfit ourselves with the full armor of God.

Faith will make us whole,

And he said unto her, Daughter, be of good comfort: thy faith hath made thee whole; go in peace. Luke 8:48.

And he said unto him, Arise, go thy way: thy faith hath made thee whole. Luke 17:19.

We, as Christians, gain experience with faith on a day to day basis. Faith has the ability to release fears and stress out of our daily lives. Without faith we are pitiful creatures who shy away from every demonic tragedy that enters our area of operations. I am no less susceptible to this lack of faith but I do have the experience that God has given me to defeat that lack. God has a habit of bringing us to a point where we finally realize that the self cannot do what needs to be done. He lets us bring certain things down on ourselves and in that "ah-ha" moment the Holy Ghost whispers, "Let me take care of it."

Listen for that whisper, child of God, and have faith that God will step in.

Recently my wife and I found ourselves in a position where we were going to lose our home. My first thought, I'm ashamed to admit, was what am I going to do about it. I tried many solutions to the problem. Worrying myself literally sick. Every door slammed shut. There was no way. We were going to be thrown out on the street. Finally when I came to my end I had no choice but to trust my God. Instead of my prayer being, "Lord let me find a way out of this mess," it changed to, "Lord let your will be done. I bow myself before you a humble and terrified man who deserves nothing of the kindness you have bestowed on me from the day I came to earth. Forgive me Father." From that day forward I could see his hand in everything that was going on around me. He delivered the funds needed to save our home but the thing that is truly important here is that even if He had not I had decided that he was able and knew more about what I needed than I. Praise God!

Warriors be faithful to God for everything. Even the little things. How many times have we been moved to a certain location because of delays in order to fulfill God's will? Stuck in traffic? Flat tire? Ever think that maybe God placed that stumbling block to guard us against danger or to place us in an area for His glory. There really is not anything that is coincidence. Just because we find ourselves in a remarkable occurrence of events that seem to have no apparent connection does not mean that your God is not directing things, indeed, it is even more suspect that He is.

What Faith is not

The first thing that faith is not is that it is not a pursuit or interest followed with some kind of devotion, ie, a religion. It is not a doctrine or an idea passed down from our ancestors. It is not some uncritical way of thinking that tell us the difference between truth and lies. Faith cannot save you,

What doth it profit, my brethren, though a man say he hath faith, and have not works? can faith save him? James 2:14.

Thou believest that there is one God; thou doest well: the devils also believe, and tremble. James 2:19,

Satan knows the truth as well as his demons. This is not confidence, only a fool says there is no God.

We will mention later that faith is definitely not a way too somehow "boss" God around. He will not be our personal attendant when what we ask for is out of His will. Faith is not magic. We cannot, through some incantation, decree what God will do. The order of reality is the exact opposite. God will decide what we will do if we allow Him to.

Faith is not synonymous with hope. Hope is a feeling of expectation. Faith is complete trust and confidence. Hope is someday. Faith is now.

What Faith is

Having faith in a living, God is to have full confidence in His truth and reliability.

Now faith is the substance of things hoped for, the evidence of things not seen. Heb. 11:1.

When a spiritual warrior has faith, he knows in his inner most being that God supports him before the situation he finds himself in even develops. Faith is solidly based in reality and fact.

For verily I say unto you, That whosoever shall say unto this mountain, Be thou removed, and be thou cast into the sea; and shall not doubt in his heart, but shall believe that those things which he saith shall come to pass; he shall have whatsoever he saith. Mark 11:23.

Faith is moral strength and power. When the warrior has faith in the words of God, he finds a door into the strength and power of the Supreme Commander. This faith must be from a warrior's very soul, not from just some mental power or intelligence. Faith is not negotiable.

For with the heart man believeth unto righteousness; and with the mouth confession is made unto salvation. Romans 10:10.

Faith is not seeing. It is not based on some Missourian thought pattern like "Show me". Things that occur in our vision don't require faith,

For we walk by faith, not by sight: 2 Cor 5:7.

14: And this is the confidence that we have in him, that, if we ask any thing according to his will, he heareth us:

15: And if we know that he hear us, whatsoever we ask, we know that we have the petitions that we desired of him. 1 John 5: 14&15.

God expects, that when we ask, that we know in our very soul that not only are our pleas answered at the moment we ask them but have been answered even before we ask. It is already a done deal.

35: Cast not away therefore your confidence, which hath great recompence of reward.

36: For ye have need of patience, that, after ye have done the will of God, ye might receive the promise. Heb. 10:35&36,

Note that we must do the will of God and not our own. Never throw away your ability to totally rely on the Supreme Commander, I speak from experience here. To be effective in this spiritual warfare we absolutely need the self-assurance that arises from our faith in God. This confidence leads to our recognition of service to Him.

That ye be not slothful, but followers of them who through faith and patience inherit the promises. Heb. 6:12.

By reading the battle manual we can have faith in experiential form seeing how God took care of those in the past. In the words of that old hymn, "What He's done for others He will do for you." God is worthy of our trust and He is the only one who has the assets that can be drawn on in order for the warrior to function effectively.

Faith is like Newton's third law of thermodynamics, For every action there is an equal and opposite reaction. When we act as we believe, with God's power and knowing His will, we will see an equal reaction to our action just as the heros of faith saw,

21: Was not Abraham our father justified by works, when he had offered Isaac his son upon the altar?

22: Seest thou how faith wrought with his works, and by works was faith made perfect?

23: And the scripture was fulfilled which saith, Abraham believed God, and it was imputed unto him for righteousness: and he was called the Friend of God. James 2:21-23.

One of my personal favorite men from history was Davy Crockett. He is attributed to the saying, "Be sure you're right then go ahead." Living in faith means just that.

Faith has the connotation of rest. Peace. If you are "trying to believe" then you just haven't got it. There is no trying with faith, fellow warriors, there is only having. There is no doing, just believing.

The battle manual explains that faith is a precious commodity,

That the trial of your faith, being much more precious than of gold that perisheth, though it be tried with fire, might be found unto praise and honour and glory at the appearing of Jesus Christ: 1 Peter 1:7.

We have already touched on persecution and every mature spiritual warrior realizes that there will be difficulties as well as blessings and that even the difficulties are blessings. The promises given to uphold your faith when you are being "tested by fire" are an important addition to your arsenal,

For God so loved the world, that he gave his only begotten Son, that whosoever believeth in him should not perish, but have everlasting life. John 3:16.

Faith carries' with it our very salvation.

And all things, whatsoever ye shall ask in prayer, believing, ye shall receive. Matt. 21:22. Faith is responsible for answered prayer.

23: For verily I say unto you, That whosoever shall say unto this mountain, Be thou removed, and be thou cast into the sea; and shall not doubt in his heart, but shall believe that those things which he saith shall come to pass; he shall have whatsoever he saith.

24: Therefore I say unto you, What things soever ye desire, when ye pray, believe that ye receive them, and ye shall have them. Mark 21:23&24.

The way that we make our spiritual warfare effective and acceptable to our Supreme Commander is by faith. Faith is one of two major components in our warfare. The other being grace.

Our Supreme Commander is the same today as yesterday and He will be the same tomorrow. (Heb. 13:8). Through His warriors God wants to show His power in a way that others can see and feel. Our testimony will not come from our speech or our writings but by the power of God.

For the kingdom of God is not in word, but in power. 1 Cor. 4:20.

How to develop faith

One

Understand that once you became a child of God you were immediately allotted a measure of faith,

For I say, through the grace given unto me, to every man that is among you, not to think of himself more highly than he ought to think; but to think soberly, according as God hath dealt to every man the measure of faith. Romans 12:3.

As spiritual warriors we need to build upon that measure. It grows within itself and our experience. Patience is at the center of faith. Wait upon God. He is sure and able. It is like when we start a fire. We start with small bits of wood known as kindling, then add larger pieces until it is ready for logs and beams.

Two

Read the battle manual,
So then faith cometh by hearing, and hearing by the word of God. Romans 10:17.
20: My son, attend to my words; incline thine ear unto my sayings.
21: Let them not depart from thine eyes; keep them in the midst of thine heart.
22: For they are life unto those that find them, and health to all their flesh. Prov. 4: 20-22.

Keeping an eye on the battle manual is THE way to add to your faith. It stops us from believing the lies that are told us by the world at all times. I think it was Joseph Goebbels who stated, "If a lie is told enough times people will begin to take it as the truth." The battle manual will stop the insidious lies that the world tells us from so many different directions. A good way to keep our battle manual in mind is to find those other spiritual warriors to keep company with. I praise God for the ones that I have found.

Obey the whispers of the Holy Spirit. He is the Supreme Commander for us in this world. Do what He says now. God will not reveal His total battle plan until we are faithful in what we are to do at this moment. Obedience to the things that the Spirit is showing you right now, either through the word or through your mind, is crucial to future action and knowledge.

Three

Never forget to give thanks for those things that the Father has bestowed on you. In every thing give thanks: for this is the will of God in Christ Jesus concerning you. 1 Thess. 5:18. Never forget to give thanks for all things! Even those things that appear to be against you. We see through a glass darkly. Our perception is clouded by the world. This is why we must choose our battles wisely with the help of the Holy Spirit.

Four

Praise and worship the Supreme Commander. Satan cannot tolerate praise for our living God and must flee. Praise is in itself an act of faith. Faith grows in the presence of praise,

By him therefore let us offer the sacrifice of praise to God continually, that is, the fruit of our lips giving thanks to his name. Heb. 13:15.

Worship is to show our admiration and devotion to the God of creation and strengthens our faith. Obviously, if we worship, our trust and love in Him are made manifest and our faith will grow. What is worship? Worship is when one loves another being, uncritically and unquestioningly. It is showing devotion to our Supreme Commander. Worship is not attending religious services. It is individualistic. Worship is reverence and love.

Praise suggests respect and admiration. Gratitude to a living God who cares for you as an individual. It is the expression of admiration for our Supreme Commander.

Five

Others who have an advanced faith should be sought out. Faith is contagious.

He that walketh with wise men shall be wise: but a companion of fools shall be destroyed. Prov. 13:20.

This does not mean that we go to "church" every Sunday. That is a fine attribute but what the spiritual warrior needs is to associate himself with other warriors who are progressing in the battle and have experience that is vital to your own growth. An experienced soldier or fighter who knows how to treat wounds. Who knows what to do when things get out of hand . Who knows how to proceed when you have come to your own end. Someone who knows how to listen to the Holy Spirit.

Six

God's battle manual is blessed and its power is released when it is recited to others. So speak it. Tell others of its magnificent action in your own life. Even the angels listen to God's word when spoken, Bless the LORD, ye his angels, that excel in strength, that do his commandments, hearkening unto the voice of his word. Psalms 103:20.

To be physically and mentally strong we need to be in the word. We are daily facing an enemy whose capability in terms of personnel and materiel is extremely strong. The spiritual warrior needs to "hit" the enemy with all the force he can muster. Our main assets are the Holy Spirit and the infallible word of God. In the word there is safety and power to withstand the enemy's attacks. These are the skills that you must become strong in to be effective. Our Commander's words have the power to show the course of action that we should pursue. Only by reading the word can we receive the power to resist the stress and force of the enemy.

Seven

Faith works by love and nothing else. The "law" does not apply, For in Jesus Christ neither circumcision availeth anything, nor uncircumcision; but faith which worketh by love. Gal.5: 6. Want a great faith? Listen to the word,

5: And when Jesus was entered into Capernaum, there came unto him a centurion, beseeching him,

6: And saying, Lord, my servant lieth at home sick of the palsy, grievously tormented.

7: And Jesus saith unto him, I will come and heal him.

8: The centurion answered and said, Lord, I am not worthy that thou shouldest come under my roof: but

speak the word only, and my servant shall be healed.

9: For I am a man under authority, having soldiers under me: and I say to this man, Go, and he goeth; and to another, Come, and he cometh; and to my servant, Do this, and he doeth it.

10: When Jesus heard it, he marvelled, and said to them that followed, Verily I say unto you, I have not found so great faith, no, not in Israel. Matt. 8:5-10.

Eight

Love will find a way.

Follow peace with all men, and holiness, without which no man shall see the Lord: Heb. 12:14.

For with the heart man believeth unto righteousness; and with the mouth confession is made unto salvation. Romans 10:10.

Try to find a pure heart. Be forgiving. Be at peace with all men if possible.

If it be possible, as much as lieth in you, live peaceably with all men. Romans 12:18.

In this way we can keep our spiritual "sight". Faith can only exist with a pure heart. A pure heart can only exist in the presence of the Holy Spirit. One of the greatest acknowledgments, in my temporary duty here on earth, was when a fellow warrior told me I have a good heart. Praise God for him.

Nine

Jude 1:20,

But ye, beloved, building up yourselves on your most holy faith, praying in the Holy Ghost.

Be filled with the Holy Spirit. Read 1 Cor. 14. We are instructed and improved morally and in our minds when we practice the gifts that God has supplied us with. Faith is the fruit of the Spirit and those that worship God need to worship Him in Spirit and in truth.

Grace

Grace is the free and unearned favor of God. In legal terms it means a period that is officially allowed for the fulfillment of an obligation. It is said that we live under the law of grace,

For sin shall not have dominion over you: for ye are not under the law, but under grace. Romans 6:14.

Paul is stating, unequivocally, that we are in the age of grace and that as the elect, if we fulfill our obligation, we have the following,

23: For all have sinned, and come short of the glory of God;

24: Being justified freely by his grace through the redemption that is in Christ Jesus: Romans 3:23&24.

I am always amazed that some churches have you memorize

Romans 3:23 but hardly ever have you memorize verse twenty-four. So what is sin? It is defined as an immoral act considered to violate the laws of God. Remember the laws of the Supreme Commander? They bear repeating. Love the Lord thy God with all your heart, soul and mind. Love thy neighbor as thyself. Go out into all the world and preach the gospel to every living creature. Well, He did say that His burden is light, Matt 11:28:30,

28: Come unto me, all ye that labour and are heavy laden, and I will give you rest.

29: Take my yoke upon you, and learn of me; for I am meek and lowly in heart: and ye shall find rest unto your souls.

30: For my yoke is easy, and my burden is light.

My dear fellow believers if you find yourself in a relationship with a church that has more rules and regulations than these three, consider a move. The battle is too important to be weighed down by excess baggage.

Romans 11:6,
And if by grace, then is it no more of works: otherwise grace is no more grace. But if it be of works, then is it no more grace: otherwise work is no more work.

Again we cannot do anything for God. Our works are only viable and only have reason if they are the works of God through us. We cannot buy our way into heaven through the works of self, indeed, the Supreme Commander requires us to deny ourselves so that He may work through us. It's grace my fellow warriors,

8: For by grace are ye saved through faith; and that not of yourselves: it is the gift of God:

9: Not of works, lest any man should boast.

10: For we are his workmanship, created in Christ Jesus unto good works, which God hath before ordained that we should walk in them. Eph. 2:8-10.

Grace is to be used for the glory of the Supreme Commander. This next passage could be this child of God's theme song,
9: For I am the least of the apostles, that am not meet to be called an apostle, because I persecuted the church of God.
10: But by the grace of God I am what I am: and his grace which was bestowed upon me was not in vain; but I laboured more abundantly than they all: yet not I, but the grace of God which was with me.
1 Cor. 15:10.
If you wish to understand just how important this grace thing is just go over the epistles in you battle manual and look at how the apostles began and ended their letters to the various churches.

Psalms 84:11 needs repeating,
For the LORD God is a sun and shield: the LORD will give grace and glory: no good thing will he withhold from them that walk uprightly.
The key for the use of all the gifts that God has chosen to outfit His saints, here on earth, is the denial of self. We cannot be an effective spiritual warrior without self-denial.
I can of mine own self do nothing: as I hear, I judge: and my judgment is just; because I seek not mine own will, but the will of the Father which hath sent me. John 5:30.
For a bishop must be blameless, as the steward of God; not self willed, not soon angry, not given to wine, no striker, not given to filthy lucre; Titus 1:7.
We need to mirror the Supreme Commander who came here to save that which was lost, by sacrifice.
God became human and gave up Himself so that the elect would share in His majesty. How can we do less?

23: And he said to them all, If any man will come after me, let him deny himself, and take up his cross daily, and follow me.

24: For whosoever will save his life shall lose it: but whosoever will lose his life for my sake, the same shall save it. Luke 9:23&24.

Whosoever shall seek to save his life shall lose it; and whosoever shall lose his life shall preserve it. Luke 17:33.

There seems to be two wrong ideas about grace that have surfaced over the millennia. Plots of the deceiver to undermine the glory of God.

What Grace is not

Grace is not freedom to do as one wishes relying on the grace of God to bridge the gap. Grace is not license. We cannot, as spiritual warriors, ignore the commandments of our Supreme Commander and count on grace to be a remedy. This " doctrine" implies that we can have an attitude of rebellion against God and live a hedonistic life style and not have it affect us because we are under grace. Remember that those commandments that the Supreme Commander gave us were not suggestions. It is vitally important that the spiritual warrior be bound by those three commandments.

This doctrine, if it results in abnormal or unacceptable behavior concerning the Supreme Commander's truths, is WRONG. He hates sin, (Psalms 5:5), He requires that it be punished, (2 Pet. 2:9). While true that grace covers a multitude of sins our Supreme Commander states that if you love Him you will follow His commandments.

Romans 6;

1: What shall we say then? Shall we continue in sin, that grace may abound?

2: God forbid. How shall we, that are dead to sin, live any longer therein?

God through Paul makes it clear what grace is not.

15: What then? shall we sin, because we are not under the law, but under grace? God forbid.

16: Know ye not, that to whom ye yield yourselves servants to obey, his servants ye are to whom ye obey; whether of sin unto death, or of obedience unto righteousness?

You as a warrior have decided whom to obey. In obedience is our righteousness.

23: For the wages of sin is death; but the gift of God is eternal life through Jesus Christ our Lord. That's what I love about the battle manual. God's promises are always kept.

But grow in grace, and in the knowledge of our Lord and Saviour Jesus Christ. To him be glory both now and for ever. Amen. 2 Peter 3:18.

Another thing that grace is not is some type of strict conformity to religious rules rather than the spirit of the commandments of our Supreme Commander. We have already gone over how to please God. This conformity is not about keeping the commandments it is about depending on Him. What I am saying here is that we cannot trust ourselves for some type of salvation through personal effort. You were never "saved" by any act of yourself. God has made that fact clear. For all have sinned and fallen short of the glory of God. Death to self and life through a living Savior is the answer.

What Grace is

We have already defined grace but I think a little more explanation is in order. In the days of the Old Testament God received animal sacrifices for the atonement of sin. I believe that my God never wanted the sacrifice. I think, above all else, He just wanted to be obeyed. His will carried out. Legally a testament is a document that declares a person's wishes regarding the disposal of their property. The property referred to in this case is US!

For by him were all things created, that are in heaven, and that are in earth, visible and invisible, whether they be thrones, or dominions, or principalities, or powers: all things were created by him, and for him: Col. 1:16.

In those "old days" God accepted the sacrifices as a stand in for the Supreme Commander. Jesus, basically, came to earth to do something that no man had done since the beginning of time, truly and wholly do the will of God,

10: By the which will we are sanctified through the offering of the body of Jesus Christ once for all.

14: For by one offering he hath perfected for ever them that are sanctified. Heb. 10:10&14.

The Supreme Commander became a man. One of us. As one of us he did, finally and fully, what God had wanted all along. A man who would perfectly do His will. And although this Man had no sin of His own, He died for ours. He traded places with us. The New Testament is the final disposition of the property of Almighty God,

18: And all things are of God, who hath reconciled us to himself by Jesus Christ, and hath given to us the ministry of reconciliation;

19: To wit, that God was in Christ, reconciling the world unto himself, not imputing their trespasses unto them; and hath committed unto us the word of reconciliation. 2Cor. 5:18&19.

That word reconciliation is a blessing on which we must hang our hats as spiritual warriors. It means to restore friendly relations between ourselves and our God. To become compatible with the Creator of the universe. It comes from the Latin root meaning "bring together." Praise God!

The Supreme Commander did nothing less than take our place on that cross of calvary. He retrieved that which He owned and gave us instance access to God,

And the sun was darkened, and the veil of the temple was rent in the midst. Luke 23:45.

When the veil was torn, it meant that we no longer needed a priest to intercede with God, Almighty.

1: There is therefore now no condemnation to them which are in Christ Jesus, who walk not after the flesh, but after the Spirit.

2: For the law of the Spirit of life in Christ Jesus hath made me free from the law of sin and death.

3: For what the law could not do, in that it was weak through the flesh, God sending his own Son in the likeness of sinful flesh, and for sin, condemned sin in the flesh:

4: That the righteousness of the law might be fulfilled in us, who walk not after the flesh, but after the Spirit. Romans 8: 1-4.(More on this passage later.)

Paul says it best. If, as a spiritual warrior, you walk after the Spirit(listen to the Holy Ghost) there is no condemnation. This means that the punishment(death) has been exorcized. YOU HAVE BEEN DECLARED TO BE FIT FOR USE BY GOD.

As spiritual warriors it is vital that we fulfill these following verses. God commands that we give up ourselves before we can be effective for the kingdom of God. In fact, only through self-denial can we gain the blessings that God has for us,

3: Blessed are the poor in spirit: for theirs is the kingdom of heaven.

4: Blessed are they that mourn: for they shall be comforted.

5: Blessed are the meek: for they shall inherit the earth.

6: Blessed are they which do hunger and thirst after righteousness: for they shall be filled.

7: Blessed are the merciful: for they shall obtain mercy.

8: Blessed are the pure in heart: for they shall see God.

9: Blessed are the peacemakers: for they shall be called the children of God.

10: Blessed are they which are persecuted for righteousness' sake: for theirs is the kingdom of heaven.

11: Blessed are ye, when men shall revile you, and persecute you, and shall say all manner of evil against you falsely, for my sake. Matthew 5 : 3-11.

Poor in spirit

I believe that our Supreme Commander is referring to those that have given up even their spirit to the will of God. Spirit means breath in the original Latin. So what He is saying are those willing to give even their breath to Him will have the kingdom. He said, " Do the whole need a physician?" The Kingdom is made up of those that have kept their faith no matter their worldly circumstances.

Mourn

Those that "mourn" are those that feel a deep sorrow following a death. I think that those that mourn the sacrifice of the Supreme Commander will be led to understand the reason for that sacrifice. In our temporary duty station we mourn for all sorts of reasons. We mourn our lot in life. Our circumstances. The things that happen to those we love. The Supreme Commander is well aware of the losses His warriors take and in Him is the comfort we seek.

Meek

Again those that quietly, and submissively come to the Father will inherit the earth. WE WIN!

Our Father is faithful and just to forgive our sins and cleanse us in righteous. If we only let Him. We must be steadfast and loyal to our Commander. He is our strength. The warrior must be habitual in his faith. He must be marked by fidelity to the living God. We must conform to the original intent of the Supreme Commander's battle orders. Steadfast in our allegiance and affection. Consistently reliable and dependable to spread the good news to the property of Almighty God. Constant in our devotion.

Hunger and thirst after righteousness

Those that search and are authentically thirsty to do that which is morally right and justifiable will be filled with the Holy Spirit. All He really wants is for us to listen for His words and obey. To hear with the intention of acting on His voice so that He might work through us to advance the battle. To perceive what He clearly means. See the error clearly that the enemy has presented to us. To hear all the evidence that He has made available to us. If you haven't heard His words recently that, in itself, is a good indication that the enemy is advancing. Listen for His voice. It is always there.

Merciful

Those that allow the Holy Ghost to give relief from suffering to their fellow man will receive relief themselves. Mercy is the basis of God's plan. Show kindness to the distressed. That is His will and it is the very foundation of our humanity. Compassion and sympathy are strong ways of fighting the enemy. Mercy is how our Supreme Commander administers justice and so should we.

Pure in heart

Believers whose hearts have not mixed their belief and dependance on God with any type of humanistic belief will understand and see God. Be free, fellow warriors, of extraneous elements that inhibit your prime directive. Without qualification or exception place your mind-body-soul in the hands of the Supreme Commander. Fight the fight with the greatest intensity. Study the word as a child for such is the Kingdom of Heaven. Keep your eyes on the prize.

Peacemakers

Those who are able to free their mind from disturbances with a tranquil knowledge and faith in God shall be called the children or even a better word, descendants of God. We are in this battle for the long run(eternity) so strive to be at peace with all men as far as you are able. Do not harbor any mental stress or anxiety but live by faith. As far as able be free from disputes with your fellow warriors. Listen to their, "word of knowledge" before discernment. There will be no peace treaty with the enemy until our Lord and Savior returns.

For His sake

Take this blessing to heart spiritual warriors. Did I happen to mention, WE WIN!

BASIC TRAINING
Part Two

What to expect as God's warrior

For every battle of the warrior is with confused noise, and garments rolled in blood; Isa. 9:5.

As I stated in the forward here's what to expect as a warrior of God. Persecution (both religious and demonic), rejection, insult, slander, discreditation, betrayal, false accusation, hatred (religious and racial), ridicule, temptation and the suffering that come from resistance.

Persecution
religious

This is not a warning it is a promise, 2 Tim.3: 12, Yea, and all that will live godly in Christ Jesus shall suffer persecution. Organized religions tend to form force fields around themselves by enacting rules. Do this, don't do that or just say no, help to reinforce that field. To be fair most of the rules were developed to make for an orderly meeting, unfortunately, what the result has become is that, the meetings require you to sit, shut up and listen. No more. No less. The thing is that spiritual warfare like earthly warfare is not orderly. It is extremely messy. You'll be all right, in such a church, as long as you follow the rules. Our Supreme Commander, on the other hand, gave us very few rules and here they are,

One

And he answering said, Thou shalt love the Lord thy God with all thy heart, and with all thy soul, and with all thy strength, and with all thy mind; and thy neighbour as thyself. Luke 10:27.

Two

And he said unto them, Go ye into all the world, and preaches the gospel to every creature. Mark 16:15.

On these two commandments hang all the law and the prophets. Matt. 22: 40.

That's it folks, any more than these three are superfluous.

The persecution comes in when you break one of those superfluous rules. You may be ignored, chastised, refused communion or excommunicated, depending on the church. In the "good old days" you might have been flogged, jailed or burned at the stake. There is something to be said to living in modern times.

Paul was both a persecutor and persecuted by the church. His answer to religious persecution?

Bless them which persecute you: bless, and curse not. Romans 12:14.

There is more religious persecution going on in this century than any other in history. We, residing in the U.S. don't see the greatest part of this persecution. (although it is here and becoming worse by the day). Terrible and brutal persecution is going on in the world around us. Thousands of believers have been killed in just the last few years. Others have been tortured, sold into slavery, starved, sent to prison and burned. Christians are the most persecuted group in the world. It is estimated that over two million Christians are currently being persecuted for their beliefs. It is my belief that we will see the same in our country in the not too distant future. Here, in the U.S., persecution resides under the so-called doctrine of the separation of church and state. Nowhere will you find this "theory" in the Constitution but it is having the same influence over our country's laws as if it existed. The Constitution reads,

Congress shall make no law respecting an establishment of religion, or prohibiting the free exercise thereof;

No prayers in school? Hate crime legislation? No Ten Commandments in public places? These are prohibiting the free exercise thereof. Continue in violation of these new laws and you will find yourself in jail. The men who started our country were quite concerned that this new government would be based on the legitimacy of the individual. They were afraid that the government would try to decree a state religion as England had done. In other words they said that this new government was to leave religion alone. They wanted it to be left to the individual.

As time has gone by and with the arrival of the separation of church and state dogma we are witnessing exactly what the founding fathers had hoped to avoid. A state run religion called humanism: A rationalistic system of thought that attaches prime importance to human matters instead of the matters of God. Make no mistake humanism is a religion.

Persecution
demonic

Demonic persecution is much harder to describe. No, your head won't spin on your shoulders. It will be much more subtle than that. The devil hates the truth and, in fact, is the father of lies. He will use lies to persecute you. He will whisper lies that you are not good enough. He will whisper lies that you're too sinful. He will sow doubts and fears.

Those by the way side are they that hear; then cometh the devil, and taketh away the word out of their hearts, lest they should believe and be saved. Luke 8:12

Fear not, here's what to do,

Submit yourselves therefore to God. Resist the devil, and he will flee from you. James 4:7.

Persecution can be allowed as discipline. It can be used to show us that our treasure here on earth is meaningless. It can show how much we have invested in our egos and personal interests and the difference between that and how much we have invested in the Supreme Commander. If we have invested more in love of things or ourselves than being loved and loving the Supreme Commander, we will be overly concerned when those investments become threatened. If we find that our "earthly" treasures are threatened the situation can produce anxiety, fear, hurt or anger. How come? "Where your treasure is, there your heart will be also," (Luke 12:34, Matthew 6:21).

Our Supreme Commander put up all His treasure with His Father and His heart naturally followed to where His treasure was. Do you ever wonder how it was that He hardly seemed concern by the continual hate and malice He received at the hands of the people around Him? He was never threatened or ever sought approval from them. He knew where His treasure was. All He cared about were the matters of His Father. All He cared about was fulfilling the Father's will and obeying Him.

"Teacher, we know you are a man of integrity. You are not swayed by men because you pay no attention to who they are; but you teach the way of God in accordance with the truth," (Mark 12:14).

As apprentices we are called to be just like Him in every way. He was cruelly murdered on that cross for the sake of the world. His persecution was a perfect example of how little he cared for His own needs. Persecution for us has meaning only if we use it to remove the vestiges of self that inhabit our soul and replace it with His selfless nature. Remember what He said to Peter,

Get behind Satan! You are a stumbling block to me; you do not have in mind the things of God, but the things of men, (Matthew 16:23).

The truth of the matter is that God leads us to areas that are designed to kill the self. The self is a hindrance to the Supreme Commander's leadership and it blocks us from our work.

This bears repeating. Depending on the self in spiritual warfare equals defeat. The only way that we can be victorious is drawing on the strength of God through prayer and the study of the battle manual. Only in this way can we come to the denial of self and the Supreme Commander's command to put the interest of others ahead of ourselves. Only in this way can we understand that the opponent we face is neither people nor circumstances but that old enemy, the devil. Remember that God only allows the enemy's attacks for the reason of refining His warriors for our battle. To have us realistically assess what our interests truly are, what our motives are and to enrich our commitment to the Supreme Commander.

It never ceases to amaze me at how angry the Supreme Commander gets at those that persecute His front line troops. Judgement is instantaneous in some cases. I have even seen the persecutors taken from this earth, under some circumstances. Then, again, one shouldn't be surprised,

"I will bless those who bless you, and whoever curses you I will curse; and all peoples on earth will be blessed through you," Genesis 12:3.

Keep in mind, at all times, that it is God who does the cursing and not us. We are required to bless not curse and vengeance is mine sayeth the Lord. He is so much better at it than we are. As warriors we are required to pray for those that would persecute us.

Rejection

This is just one of the lies that will be whispered in your ear. You will be dismissed as inadequate. There will be some who refuse to consider what you are saying or agree to your premises. Perhaps the worse is that the people you count on most will fail to show you affection or concern.

Know this, if you are rejected our Supreme Commander was rejected before you. He was rejected by his religion, He was rejected by His culture and He was rejected by His people and here is what He said,

And have ye not read this scripture; The stone which the builders rejected is become the head of the corner: Mark 10:12.

Possibly nothing hurts more than rejection from the body of Christ. Those that have become steeped in law and rules. Those that leave you when they are needed most. Make no mistake, it is declared that you listen to a word of knowledge when it is spoken to you by fellow believer's but you need discernment. Listen foremost to the Holy Spirit. He will never steer you wrong. If the words you hear are in direct opposition to what the Spirit is saying, I think you know which to follow. Remember that even His most loyal apostles turned on the Supreme Commander.

Insult

You will be abused and disrespected. Know that the Supreme Commander was abused both physically and emotionally. He was not respected by the very people He came here to suffer and die for.

The religious people of Jesus's day claimed that He was in league with Satan and that He cast out devils' in the devil's name. What a tragic insult to the King of Kings. What an offense. A statement so contemptible to our Supreme Commander.

Once when I ran for school board, I was called a Nazi in a letter, to the editor, in a local newspaper. What an insult. A sense of humor helps. I wrote back that I didn't know I was a Nazi. I thought, instead, that I was a Baptist.

Slander

They will try to damage your reputation. All manner of false accusations will be made about you. As I said in the above paragraph, I have been called a Nazi. I have also been called a heretic, a drug dealer and worse. I wear those tags as I would medals of honor. Long before I began my own battles in spiritual warfare, my Supreme Commander was called even worse. The fact is each one of you is an individual and my Jesus works on the individual heart. Be who you are. Open up to the Supreme Commander so that He can work through you. Hold on, it will be a bumpy ride. Did I mention, "WE WIN?"

Discreditation

They will try and cause your evidence or ideas to seem false or unreliable. The way to combat this is to make sure that your ideas are proven by our battle manual. The Holy Spirit will not fail you. Listen to His words. Allow Him to open the doors and to bring you into His circle of influence.

Betrayal

Some will aid the enemy by acting treacherously toward you or by revealing information about you. Expect disloyalty. Here's what the Supreme Commander told Peter,

But when he had turned about and looked on his disciples, he rebuked Peter, saying, Get thee behind me, Satan: for thou savourest not the things that be of God, but the things that be of men. Mark 8:33.

False accusation

There may be some who will charge or claim that you have done something illegal or wrong. I can tell you right now that this is one of the things that you will face in spiritual warfare. The enemy will use this against you just as he used it against our Supreme Commander.

And the chief priests and scribes stood and vehemently accused him. Luke 23:10.

Paul, also, was falsely accused,

Whom I perceived to be accused of questions of their law, but to have nothing laid to his charge worthy of death or of bonds. Acts 23:29.

In these days recent history is resplendent with spiritual warriors being falsely accused of child abuse, money laundering, drug abuse and other sundry crimes. When this occurs there is a solution,

11: And when they bring you unto the synagogues, and unto magistrates, and powers, take ye no thought how or what thing ye shall answer, or what ye shall say:

12: For the Holy Ghost shall teach you in the same hour what ye ought to say. Luke 12: 11&12.

Hatred

There will be those from the religious side that will feel an intense dislike for you simply because you are a warrior. They spend their days sitting and listening but they have never set out to fight the enemy as you have. They are motivated by prejudice. The Baptists hate the Methodists. The Methodists hate the Pentecostal and so forth.

Satan hates you. He is out to try and get you to die. Satan will try and steal your soul. He will try to destroy your belief. Here's what the Supreme Commander had to say,

If the world hate you, ye know that it hated me before it hated you. John 15:18.

Blessed are ye, when men shall hate you, and when they shall separate you from their company, and shall reproach you, and cast out your name as evil, for the Son of man's sake. Luke 6:22.

But I say unto you which hear, Love your enemies, do good to them which hate you, Luke 6:27.

And ye shall be hated of all men for my name's sake. Luke 21:17.

Ridicule

No one likes to be made the butt of jokes or to be mocked but that is what you have to look forward to. "That crazy Christian always spouting off on how God does this or that." Remember that they called our Supreme Commander a devil. There is a myriad of sundry jokes about men of God none of which need to be repeated here. Suffice it to say that we need that, " Breastplate of Righteousness" to survive those slings and arrows.

Temptation

We all have inclinations or urges. Certain things of the world have an allure that beckons us to do something against our better judgement. The devil uses this allure. We all have desires and the devil will use those desires against us but, as a child of God, there is a promise,

There hath no temptation taken you but such as is common to man: but God is faithful, who will not suffer you to be tempted above that ye are able; but will with the temptation also make a way to escape, that ye may be able to bear it. 1 Cor. 10:13.

Suffering that comes from resistance

Bad and unpleasant things can happen at any time but especially if we are resisting the devil. Paul explained the phenomena in Romans 5 : 3&4,

3: And not only so, but we glory in tribulations also: knowing that tribulation worketh patience;
4: And patience, experience; and experience, hope:
Did I mention, WE WIN!

A Word about Suffering

While there is suffering while resisting the devil we must take care not to make suffering our personal gospel. Since the inception of the world Satan has used sickness and disease against the Supreme Commander's warriors. The devil has oppressed them with poverty. Some won't even fight back. Some have made this suffering their main doctrine. They can even be under the delusion that their problems are some type of, unscriptural, suffering for Jesus.

We, on the other hand, should know by now that we are CONQUERORS! Romans 8:37,

Nay, in all these things we are more than conquerors through him that loved us.

We are over comers,

For whatsoever is born of God overcometh the world: and this is the victory that overcometh the world, even our faith. 1 John 5:4.

Here's a warning. Watch out. Some Christians become quite defensive about this particular doctrine. The doctrine has been repeated from the beginning and passed down over the generations. In some instances it can be seen as a somewhat logical progression. When those in the Body of Christ were being thrown to the lions or burnt at the stake it became easy to think that they were suffering for Christ. I think, though, that you can imagine how the sermons were going in those troubled times. They were focused on suffering and persecution.

The "new" Christians were ignorant of God's power and His ability to protect them. They were unaware of His ability to deliver them from those in power. Their faith was to endure the persecution without denying the Supreme Commander. This is still true today and in many parts of the world you can still lose your life for simply not denying the Creator of the universe. The trouble is, when not in these circumstances, the doctrine goes on. It becomes the primary focus of their religion.

We see this today, after a Christian warrior has fought a skirmish or battle and has won he has terrific difficulty, refocusing. Now that the battle is over and done with, what do I pray about? It is a snare that the devil uses when he lies and tells the warrior that now he must glorify God through more suffering. This is not Bible based and the two types of suffering are not the same thing. There is no comparing death for refusing to deny the Supreme Commander and sickness or poverty.

This "doctrine" supposes that since God runs and controls all, the suffering is allowed by God.

It is a punishment for some supposed sin or correction for some miss step. The warrior is being given the opportunity to demonstrate his trust and faith or as a way to grow spiritually.

The doctrine sounds very biblical, but is it? We have already seen that the devil uses the word of God for his own agenda. Satan is the father of all lies and here is a prime example. This "doctrine" places the warrior in a position where he stops resisting Satan. Instead of the ruler of this world the warrior begins to blame God for his suffering.

Let's look at the results of this demonic doctrine. It can lead first to unnecessary suffering. The idea that God has abandoned the warrior. Hypocrisy, in other words, believing that the suffering is from God but trying to find relief from it by embracing the world. It is extremely hard to have faith in God when the warrior believes that it is He who is causing his suffering. In the end this doctrine can cause the warrior to take himself out of the fight and at worse can cause the warrior's premature death.

Here's what's wrong with the demonic doctrine. My Bible tells me that God my Father is on His throne and the Supreme Commander occupies a seat on His right hand. Only His Holy Spirit resides here on earth in each of His warriors. We know, already, who the ruler of the earth is. Don't we?

Now here is what the Bible tells us about the Holy Spirit. He is here on earth to be our teacher, our comforter, our spokesman, our counselor, our reminder and the provider of divine gifts and power.

Teacher

For the Holy Ghost shall teach you in the same hour what ye ought to say. Luke 12:12.

Comforter

But the Comforter, which is the Holy Ghost, whom the Father will send in my name, he shall teach you all things, and bring all things to your remembrance, whatsoever I have said unto you. John 14:26.

Spokesman

And when they agreed not among themselves, they departed, after that Paul had spoken one word, Well spake the Holy Ghost by Esaias the prophet unto our fathers,

Counselor

Wherein God, willing more abundantly to shew unto the heirs of promise the immutability of his counsel, confirmed it by an oath: Heb. 6:17.

The word counselor has three meanings:

One

Someone who gives advice about personal problems.

33: Therefore being by the right hand of God exalted, and having received of the Father the promise of the Holy Ghost, he hath shed forth this, which ye now see and hear.

34: For David is not ascended into the heavens: but he saith himself, The LORD said unto my Lord, Sit thou on my right hand,

35: Until I make thy foes thy footstool. Acts 2:33-35.

Two

Someone who has supervisory duties.

Until the day in which he was taken up, after that he through the Holy Ghost had given commandments unto the apostles whom he had chosen: Acts 1:2.

Three

A lawyer who pleads cases in a court of law.

11: And when they bring you unto the synagogues, and unto magistrates, and powers, take ye no thought how or what thing ye shall answer, or what ye shall say:

12: For the Holy Ghost shall teach you in the same hour what ye ought to say. Luke 12:11&12.

Reminder

15: And as I began to speak, the Holy Ghost fell on them, as on us at the beginning.

16: Then remembered I the word of the Lord, how that he said, John indeed baptized with water; but ye shall be baptized with the Holy Ghost. Acts 11:15&16.

Divine Gifts
And they were all filled with the Holy Ghost, and began to speak with other tongues, as the Spirit gave them utterance. Acts 2:4.

Power

And the angel answered and said unto her, The Holy Ghost shall come upon thee, and the power of the Highest shall overshadow thee: therefore also that holy thing which shall be born of thee shall be called the Son of God. Luke 1:35.

The truth of the matter is that the Father and the Supreme

Commander have already done all that they are going to do until my Jesus returns. The Supreme Commander has already taken on the curse of sin and death. He has already taken on all this and paid the full penalty. He has atoned for ALL of the curse. Jesus has already defeated Satan.

The Supreme Commander then relinquished all duties to the Holy Spirit who promotes the system that Jesus put into place to train and equip the elect.

Delegation is the name of the game here. God delegated the running of His church to the Supreme Commander and the Supreme Commander delegated the running of His church to us through the Holy Spirit.

The suffering doctrine has another, glaring, problem. It supposes that God can do anything He wants up to and including lying and breaking His promises.

Is God sovereign? Yes sir. He is. The problem that this doctrine has is that God has made a lot of promises and brother warrior, HE KEEPS HIS PROMISES.

God is not a man, that he should lie; neither the son of man, that he should repent: hath he said, and shall he not do it? or hath he spoken, and shall he not make it good? Numbers 23:19.

One other problem that this "demonic doctrine" has is that it assumes that man cannot know or understand the will of God but just the opposite is true according to our battle manual.

Having made known unto us the mystery of his will, according to his good pleasure which he hath purposed in himself: Eph.1:9.

Wherefore be ye not unwise, but understanding what the will of the Lord is. Eph.5:17.

The "will" of God is easy to understand and as a matter of fact one is foolish if he cannot fathom that will. In addition Paul says that we should be doing the will of God from our hearts,

Servants, be obedient to them that are your masters according to the flesh, with fear and trembling, in singleness of your heart, as unto Christ; Not with eyeservice, as menpleasers; but as the servants of Christ, doing the will of God from the heart; Eph. 6:5&6.

Paul tells us that we can be filled with the knowledge of God's will,

For this cause we also, since the day we heard it, do not cease to pray for you, and to desire that ye might be filled with the knowledge of his will in all wisdom and spiritual understanding; Col. 1:9.

That we can stand complete in that will,

Epaphras, who is one of you, a servant of Christ, saluteth you, always labouring fervently for you in prayers, that ye may stand perfect and complete in all the will of God. Col 4:12.

There is a promise associated with the will of God,

For ye have need of patience, that, after ye have done the will of God, ye might receive the promise.

Heb.10:36.

We can accomplish anything if it is in the will of God, 1 John 5:14&15.

14: And this is the confidence that we have in him, that, if we ask any thing according to his will, he heareth us:

15: And if we know that he hear us, whatsoever we ask, we know that we have the petitions that we desired of him.

In the will of God we have eternal life,

Those that do the will of God will last forever, 1 John 2:7.

Those that are following along are probably chomping at the bit by this time, I can hear you all now, man, this will of God sounds really important but I'm still not sure what it is. Don't worry this is a training manual and now you're in for some serious training.

Okay recruits get this and digest it, THE WORD OF GOD IS THE BIBLE!

God is Good. Everything that He does is good. The only one that the Bible talks about as evil is Satan. The only one who comes to steal, kill and destroy is Satan. God only gives good things to His children. Satan is the enemy and don't ever forget it.

Okay now that we have made this distinction I would be amiss if I didn't say a few things about another BIG lie that Satan uses to tempt God's warriors.

The Prosperity Gospel

The other side of the coin is known as the prosperity gospel or word of faith movement. This "movement" came out of the Charismatic/Pentecostal faiths sometime ago. The theology of the movement is basically a mix of orthodox Christianity and mysticism. Those that practice word of faith believe that they can somehow manipulate faith and actually create health and wealth. They believe that these words of faith can be manipulated independently of God's will. In the final analysis they believe that God, Himself, is subject to these words of faith.

The movement can entrap the warrior who truly believes that God only wants good things for His children but this belief is not valid in its Biblical view or its theology. Here are the differences:

Word of faith does not believe that God is sovereign, in other words, the system denies God of having supreme and ultimate authority. It denies Him of His independence and accuses God of not being able to act without outside interference. The Bible says that God is sovereign,

15: For he saith to Moses, I will have mercy on whom I will have mercy, and I will have compassion on whom I will have compassion.
16: So then it is not of him that willeth, nor of him that runneth, but of God that sheweth mercy. Romans 9:15&16.

Here are the prosperity gospel's thoughts on the Supreme Commander, they believe that you can control my Jesus with their words. They believe that Jesus is dependant on them speaking Him into exsistance. Our battle manual has a different view,

14: And unto the angel of the church of the Laodiceans write; These thing's saith the Amen, the faithful and true witness, the beginning of the creation of God;
17: Because thou sayest, I am rich, and increased with goods, and have need of nothing; and knowest not that thou art wretched, and miserable, and poor, and blind, and naked: Rev. 3: 14&17.

They also have a much different outlook on the sacrifice that Jesus made for all of us. Somehow they believe that our Supreme Commander died on the cross then descended into hell, was held by Satan for three days then released on some type of technicality. They actually believe that Jesus was born again. Here's the truth;

19: But with the precious blood of Christ, as of a lamb without blemish and without spot:
20: Who verily was foreordained before the foundation of the world, but was manifest in these last times for you, 1 Pet. 1:19&20.

Our Supreme Commander never stepped into hell,

42: And he said unto Jesus, Lord, remember me when thou comest into thy kingdom.
43: And Jesus said unto him, Verily I say unto thee, To day shalt thou be with me in paradise. Luke 23: 42&43.

Neither Jesus nor Satan was in hell. He didn't need to do anything else and He stated that fact,

When Jesus therefore had received the vinegar, he said, It is finished: and he bowed his head, and gave up the ghost. John 19:30.

The prosperity gospel adherents believe that man is just a lesser god. Instead of a little lower than the angels they think that man is divine in his own right. The battle manual puts the question in a different light,

Ye are my witnesses, saith the LORD, and my servant whom I have chosen: that ye may know and believe me, and understand that I am he: before me there was no God formed, neither shall there be after me. Isa. 43:10.

In addition the word of faith believers thinks that faith is some type of force that can be manipulated to give us all of our desires. That some type of word of faith can summons up the "Spirit of life" to do our bidding from our studies, so far, we know this is a lie,

Now faith is the substance of things hoped for, the evidence of things not seen. Heb. 11:1.

I have no doubt that they are saying words that can summons up something but it is surly not a spirit of life. A synonym for faith is being sure. The surety of trusting in the promises of God our savior.

BASIC TRAINING
Part Three

The Full Armor of God

Essential equipment for the battle is listed in Eph.6:11-17. The essentials are, covering for the loins, the breastplate, shoes, shield, helmet and sword. Let's go over each separately so that the new recruit will be fully aware of the protection he needs for the battlefield. The preceding verses should be emphasized before we put any study into the actual armor for a fuller understanding of just whom this battle is against. Sun Zu in his famous book, "The Art of War," paraphrased, states that knowing yourself and you may win a small percentage of your battles...knowing the enemy and you may win half of your battles...but knowing yourself and the enemy you will win most of your battles. Fortunately Paul explains fully just who the enemy is,

"12" For we wrestle not against flesh and blood, but against principalities, against powers, against the rulers of the darkness of this world, against spiritual wickedness in high places.

13: Wherefore take unto you the whole armour of God, that ye may be able to withstand in the evil day, and having done all, to stand.

So we have to plan for a four-prong attack, keeping in mind the first sentence. We are not at war with people, indeed, people are our reason for existence. Jesus sent us on this quest to change people's hearts and by this change the world. It is vitally important that we are not mislead into thinking that various people are the enemy. Although the devil does use certain individuals just as God does we need to strike the root, as Henry David Thoreau would say. We do not "kill the messenger." So who is the enemy?

Principalities, powers, rulers of the darkness of this world and wickedness in high places. These are the enemies. Paul, here, is describing the hierarchy of the devil with all his cohorts. The devil believes that he is the god of this world and there is truth to his claim, remember he offered all the kingdoms of the world to Jesus when he was tempting Him. The devil controls a host of highly placed individuals and various cannon fodder that he uses to oppress the people of the earth through a five-step program of oppression, influence, obsession, possession and depression. We will go into depth on these subjects in a later chapter.

Covering for the loins

Stand therefore, having your loins girt about with truth.
Just what is this truth that Paul refers to? Jesus has told us plainly, In John 17:17 Jesus says, "Sanctify them through Thy truth: Thy Word is truth.

So, dear children of God, we know that the truth is the word of God. In order to fight this good fight we must have a firm grounding in the Holy Scriptures. We need to learn the sayings and instruction of our leader, Jesus Christ, in order to accurately field our weapons and to gain the field support that we desperately need. You needn't fight these battles alone. There are millions of others in the fight with you. We have already looked into just how they all fit in. For now, don't feel alone.

Truth is conformity with the facts and with reality. We all know just what this reality is. Jesus Christ, the same today as yesterday and the same tomorrow. God is truth and the truth will set you free. The thing about truth is that it is the truth whether you choose to believe it or not. There is no " situational truth" there is only truth.

Jesus saith unto him, I am the way, the truth, and the life: no man cometh unto the Father, but by me.

John 14:6.

Truth is life. Truth guards us and allows us to share in the power of Almighty God.

The Breastplate

The breastplate of righteousness. What is that? We find the description here,

For he hath made him to be sin for us, who knew no sin; that we might be made the righteousness of God in him. 2 Corinthians 2:21.

You have the protection of God with the righteousness that was bestowed on you through grace by Jesus Christ. Grace is a hard idea for some people to grasp. Simply put this is the righteousness of God that was given you the moment your heart was opened to His sacrifice, it was freely given, totally unearned, a gift that we all,as followers, have received. In legal terms it refers to being found innocent. Forgiven.

Far too many of us walk around with our main thrust being that we are unworthy worms who deserve nothing and the enemy uses this tactic to try and pierce our hearts. To keep us in unending torment. He uses ridicule, unrest, obsessions, depression and a host of other tactics to discourage the elect. Foremost he uses lies for he is the chief of all liars, but here is the truth and the basis for that breastplate. When one accepts Jesus and His sacrifice, when one realizes that in order for man to live someone had to die and when a man comes to grips with the reality that Jesus overcame death and the tomb you are instilled with a righteousness that cannot be diluted or depressed. YOU, my friend, are a SAINT! YOU are a CHILD OF GOD with all the attributes of a son, inheritance, gifts, unqualified love and devotion! YOU have direct access to the CREATOR OF THE UNIVERSE! YOU are in a RELATIONSHIP WITH GOD, ALMIGHTY! Through faith, YOU are INDESTRUCTIBLE! So put on that breastplate and act like who you are.

Shoes

If you were preparing to go into an earthly battle, you would be outfitted with combat boots that fit well and kept out the rain and cold. These boots would be equipped with steel reenforcement in order to protect the feet from incidental wounds because a battle field is really messy and the battlefields of spiritual warfare are no exception. Well God has prepared a similar shoe for your spiritual battle one that is made for the gospel of peace.

Now here's your marching order clearly laid out.

Luke 4:18-19 The Spirit of the Lord is upon me, because he hath anointed me (the Anointed One, the Messiah) to preach the gospel (good news) to the poor; he hath sent me to heal the brokenhearted, to preach deliverance (release) to the captives, and recovery of sight to the blind, to [set at liberty] (send out as delivered) those who are oppressed (bruised, trampled and stepped on, crushed and broken down by calamity) to preach (proclaim) the acceptable, (and accepted) year of the Lord [the day when salvation and the free favors of God profusely abound (Isa 61:1-2)]. Then He said, "Today this scripture has been fulfilled, here and now!"

What could be more important? The poor, desperately, need good news. Can you imagine any nobler cause than healing the brokenhearted and releasing captives that are held in the chains of depression and guilt? To bring sight to those who cannot see? To deliver out of bondage those who have been oppressed all their lives? To be accepted by the one true God of the universe? People need the Lord!

My Jesus didn't preach that God was mad and in His anger He was about to smite you down into a charred corpse. He didn't preach that if you sinned you would immediately die and be sent to hell. Jesus simplified, love the Lord your God with all your heart, mind and soul and love your neighbor as yourself. Your faith has set you free. Today you shall be with me in paradise. Go and do likewise.

The Shield

The shield of faith is essential. What is faith? Fortunately Paul comes to our rescue,

Heb 11:1 Says that faith is the substance of things hoped for, the evidence of things not seen

Faith is the foundation. Without faith we flounder in hopelessness. With faith all things are possible.

Mark 11:23. Now listen, I telling you the absolute truth here, That whoever shall say directly to this mountain, (problem, situation, disease, etc.) "Mountain, Get out of my way, and go jump in the lake!"; and will not doubt in his heart, but will have faith that what he said will happen; he will have whatever he said.

Mark 11:24 Therefore I say unto you, What things soever ye desire, when ye pray, believe that ye receive them, and ye shall have them.

The important thing here to remember is that your faith allows God to do His work and He should receive the glory. A trap the enemy uses is when we become the center piece. When we receive the glory.

The Helmet

The devil knows that to steal your resolve he needs to get into your mind so that he can use the normal desires and lusts of the "old man" to destroy us. Face it, troopers, he doesn't want you around. You are trouble for him. You represent God's work here on earth. The devil is trying to destroy you. An old Chinese saying states, where the mind goes the body follows.

Behold, God is my salvation; I will trust, and not be afraid: for the LORD JEHOVAH is my strength and my song; he also is become my salvation. Isa. 12:2.

So put on that helmet of salvation. The knowledge you have gained from your study of the Supreme Commander's words. Again you are an emissary. A protected individual. A child of the living God.

The Sword

The sword of the spirit is defined right there in Ephesians 6. It is the word of God and the sword of God is a two-edged sword. It cuts two ways. The word both slices into the enemy rendering him wounded and scarred and it also tends and heals our own wounds and the wounds of others.

God understands the lusts of our flesh and the temptations that the enemy sets before us. He has given us His battle manual and the Holy Spirit to protect us while performing our temporary duty.

12:For the word of God is quick, and powerful, and sharper than any twoedged sword, piercing even to the dividing asunder of soul and spirit, and of the joints and marrow, and is a discerner of the thoughts and intents of the heart.

13: Neither is there any creature that is not manifest in his sight: but all things are naked and opened unto the eyes of him with whom we have to do. Heb. 4:12&13.

The battle manual sets us on the right path and is the finished work of our struggle. Praise God!

6: Humble yourselves therefore under the mighty hand of God, that he may exalt you in due time:

7: Casting all your care upon him; for he careth for you.

8: Be sober, be vigilant; because your adversary the devil, as a roaring lion, walketh about, seeking whom he may devour:

9: Whom resist stedfast in the faith, knowing that the same afflictions are accomplished in your brethren that are in the world.

10: But the God of all grace, who hath called us unto his eternal glory by Christ Jesus, after that ye have suffered a while, make you perfect, stablish, strengthen, settle you.

11: To him be glory and dominion for ever and ever. Amen. 1 Pet. 5:6-11.

There is one more piece of armour that we should discuss and that is the armour of light. The Supreme Commander is the light of the world.

The night is far spent, the day is at hand: let us therefore cast off the works of darkness, and let us put on the armour of light. Romans 13:12.

8: For ye were sometimes darkness, but now are ye light in the Lord: walk as children of light:

9: (For the fruit of the Spirit is in all goodness and righteousness and truth;)

10: Proving what is acceptable unto the Lord. Eph. 5:8-10.

And what are the fruits of the Spirit?

22: But the fruit of the Spirit is love, joy, peace, longsuffering, gentleness, goodness, faith,

23: Meekness, temperance: against such there is no law. Gal. 5:22.

Love

I have gone into the attributes of love elsewhere but there is a difference between human love and the love of the Supreme Commander. We are all aware of that intense feeling of deep affection that is exhibited in us. The great interest and pleasure that we can have for certain people and things. These are emotions that we all have and are a part of our temporary duty here on earth. There is an old proverb that epitomizes how the Supreme Commander loves, He loved us enough to die for us, accepting everything about us, even our faults and weaknesses. "No greater love has a man then to lay his life down for his friends."

Joy

Joy is the feeling of great pleasure and happiness that the Spirit brings to us despite the cares of this world. The cause of joy does not always manifests itself in ways that we can understand. Through our deepest trials and tribulations joy can come unexpectedly to the spiritual warrior. Great pleasure brings joy with it as we begin to understand what God is doing with us. This emotion of great happiness can come at the most surprising of times and makes the heart glad.

Peace

Peace is more than the simple opposite of war or unrest. It is freedom. Freedom from disturbances. The tranquility found in the healing wings of our Saviour. Free from the anxiety and stress that surround us constantly. Peace denotes being reconciled with the Prince of Peace and remaining silent to hear the words of the Spirit. Through meditation we attempt to eliminate mental stress and anxiety. In doing so we try to bring into balance harmonious relations with the Supreme Commander by letting Him work through us.

Longsuffering

Longsuffering does not mean suffering long. What it does mean is patience. The capacity of the spiritual warrior to tolerate delays and trouble without becoming angry or upset. God knows what He's doing, child of God, and if God suddenly feels far away...Guess who moved?

Gentleness

The opposite of gentleness is rough and violent. As warriors we cannot be harsh or severe to those we are trying to free from oppression. There was an expression, years ago, used by soldiers in Viet Nam,

" We're here to win your hearts and minds or we'll burn your hut down."

Needless to say, to be effective spiritual warriors, this tactic will cause our failure. Be mild and kind to all those you come into contact with as well you are able. The word gentleness comes from the Old French it means " high-born or noble". Never forget who you represent. Our King.

Goodness

Goodness refers to what is valuable or useful also what is of moral excellence or admirable. Weigh that which is good against the bad. Listen to the Spirit not to men.

Faith

We have gone into this fruit of the Spirit at length but it bears repeating, have complete confidence in the Supreme Commander.

Meekness

Be submissive to the Spirit. Be quiet and gentle in His presence. Meet with Him in humility.

Temperance

Temperance means to restrain yourself. Abstaining from excesses. Paul explained it best in first Corinthians 6:12,

All things are lawful unto me, but all things are not expedient: all things are lawful for me, but I will not be brought under the power of any.

There is no law that can amend these fruits of the Spirit.

BASIC TRAINING
Part Four

Physical Education

When you join the service one of the important components of basic training is physical education or P.E. for short. It is no different in spiritual warfare's boot camp. God said, "Let us make man in our image," Gen 1:26. What does that mean? God has three distinct parts; body, soul and spirit and so have we. All three components need to be exercised.

Body

12: All things are lawful unto me, but all things are not expedient: all things are lawful for me, but I will not be brought under the power of any.
13: Meats for the belly, and the belly for meats: but God shall destroy both it and them. Now the body is not for fornication, but for the Lord; and the Lord for the body. 1 Cor. 6-12&13.

The battle you're about to enter is a battle that taxes all your components. A toned and fit body is a good first step. The enemy, as I've stated before, will attack your health. Now I am not saying that a person cannot be effective if ill or unfit. I can think of a thousand examples of people who are fighting the battle from a wheel chair or a hospital bed but for those that are not in those situations it is vital to keep the "temple of God" in the best shape it can be. You needn't spend all your waking hours in a gym and run marathons in your spare time, indeed, that time is needed for the battle. As Paul said, "all things in moderation" Keeping the temple fit just requires a few basic ideas. Get your rest. Retreat from time to time. Foremost; Relax. Remember WE WIN!

Soul

The soul is the oldest part of us. How do I know that? The Bible tells me so. The Bible says that God knew us from the foundations of the world. Genesis 2: 7 states that He breathed into his nostrils the breath of life and man became a living soul. One of my favorite philosophical sayings is, "You can never die because you have never lived. You have just forgotten who you are." It is vital to the health of our soul to remember that we have been around from the foundations of the world. This earth is just a temporary duty station and we all return to our true home in due time.

Listen to the words of the Supreme Commander, Matthew 10:28, "Fear not them which kill the body, but are not able to kill the soul: but rather fear him which is able to destroy both soul and body in hell." Sounds as if we better keep that soul fit but how do we do that?

Luke 21:19, "In your patience posses ye your souls."

Patience is defined as good nature. Wait on the Lord. Realize that like a fly on a Monet painting all we see is an undefined blob of paint. We are incapable of seeing God's big picture. This is where faith comes in. The word tells us that He knew us from the foundations of the world. Therefore, logic would require that He knows everything about us. How we will react in certain situations, what we need for the battle facing us and just where we might be situated to do the most good in this battle. The Supreme Commander has already covered this in depth,

Matt. 6: 25-34, "Therefore I say unto you, Take no thought for your life, what ye shall eat or what you should drink; nor yet for your body, what ye shall put on. Is not the life more than meat and the body than raiment? Behold the fowls of the air: for they sow not, neither do they reap, nor gather into barns; yet your heavenly Father feedeth them. Are ye not much better than they? Which of you by taking thought can add one cubit unto his stature? And why take ye thought for raiment? Consider the lilies of the field, how they grow; they toil not, neither do they spin: And yet I say unto you that even Solomon in all his glory was not arrayed like one of these. Wherefore, if God so clothe the grass of the field, which to day is, and tomorrow is cast into the oven, shall He not much more clothe you. O ye of little faith? Therefore take no thought, saying, What shall we eat, or, What shall we drink? Or, Wherewithal shall we be clothed? (For after all these things do the Gentiles seek:) for your heavenly Father knoweth that ye have need of all these things.

Now He goes on to tell us what our soul should be seeking to keep fit.

But seek ye first the kingdom of God and his righteousness: and all these things shall be added unto you. Take, therefore no thought for the morrow: for the morrow shall take thought for the things of itself. Sufficient unto the day is the evil thereof.

Exercising the soul requires faith. Not in ourselves but in the Supreme Commander. We'll study this again in logistics.

Spirit

Saint Paul covers the spirit and how to exercise it quite nicely in Romans 8 but it is useful before we go into the passage to define spirit. The Supreme Commander defines just what spirit is in John 4: 24, "God is a spirit: and they that worship Him must worship Him in spirit and in truth."

Now here's the exercise program from Saint Paul: Romans 8: 1-10,

There is therefore now no condemnation to them which are in Jesus Christ, who walk not after the flesh, but after the spirit.

This is God's promise now here is how to exercise to fulfil that promise:

1. First realize that we are free from the law of sin and death. Verse two. 2. Fulfil the righteousness of the law. Verse four. 3. Follow the ways of the Spirit. Verse five. 4. Be spiritually minded. Verse six. 5. Let the spirit of God dwell in you. Verse nine. 6. Realize that the spirit is life. Verse ten.

If properly exercised, the spirit will lead us in all things pertaining to life and especially on the battlefield. Now here's the clincher. The promise of God through Paul:

For as many as are led by the Spirit of God, they also are the SONS OF GOD. For ye have not received the spirit of bondage again to fear; but ye have received the Spirit of adoption, whereby we cry, Abba, (the Hebrew word for papa) Father. Romans 8:14&15. Got it?

Here is what the Supreme Commander says about the six ways to exercise the spirit:

1: John 5:24, "Verily, verily(this is the true truth) I say unto you, He that heareth my word, and believeth on Him that sent me, hath everlasting life, and shall not come into condemnation; but is passed from death unto life."

2:" But seek ye first the kingdom of God, and His righteousness…"

3: John 14:6, "I am the way the truth and the life. No man comes to the Father but by me."

4: Luke 12:29-31, "And seek not ye what ye shall eat, or what ye shall drink, neither are ye of doubtful mind. For all these things do the nations of the world seek after: and your Father knoweth that ye have need of these things. But rather seek ye the kingdom of God;……."

5: John 14:17, "Even the spirit of truth; whom the world cannot receive, because it seeth Him not, neither knoweth Him: but ye know Him; for He dwelleth in you, and shall be in you."

6: John 6:35, "And Jesus said unto them, I am the bread of life: he that cometh to me shall never hunger: and he that believeth in me shall never thrist."

BASIC TRAINING
Part Five

Tactics and Strategy

Tactics is defined as an action or strategy planned to achieve a specified end. It is a form of organization meant to dispose of an armed force. Strategy, on the other hand, is the art of planning and directing military activity in a war or battle. Victory is the chosen, final, outcome. We are admonished in 1 Samuel 2:3,

Talk no more so exceeding proudly; let not arrogancy come out of your mouth: for the LORD is a God of knowledge, and by him actions are weighed.

Again and I can't emphasize this enough. God is our knowledge. He is our protector. The Lord is our life and the reason for our being. He is the source of our victory.

But thanks be to God, which giveth us the victory through our Lord Jesus Christ. 1 Cor. 15:57.

For whatsoever is born of God overcometh the world: and this is the victory that overcometh the world, even our faith. 1 John 5:4.

Know thy enemy

As I stated before our enemy is Satan, the devil, lucifer.
In order to have a clear picture of how God will work through us

to defeat his works, we need to have a basic understanding of this creature.

So where does this Satan come from and what is he up too?

And the LORD said unto Satan, Whence comest thou? Then Satan answered the LORD, and said, From going to and fro in the earth, and from walking up and down in it. Job 1:7.

We know that Satan is here on earth and we know that he goes about as a lion seeking whom he can devour. He is bent on destruction.

Satan can transform himself,

And no marvel; for Satan himself is transformed into an angel of light. 1 Cor 11:14.

Satan is the father of all lies,

Ye are of your father the devil, and the lusts of your father ye will do. He was a murderer from the beginning, and abode not in the truth, because there is no truth in him. When he speaketh a lie, he speaketh of his own: for he is a liar, and the father of it. John 8:44.

The adversary would be as God,

12: How art thou fallen from heaven, O Lucifer, son of the morning! how art thou cut down to the ground, which didst weaken the nations!

13: For thou hast said in thine heart, I will ascend into heaven, I will exalt my throne above the stars of God: I will sit also upon the mount of the congregation, in the sides of the north:

14: I will ascend above the heights of the clouds; I will be like the most High. Isa. 14:12-14.

Satan can influence us through lies.

But Peter said, Ananias, why hath Satan filled thine heart to lie to the Holy Ghost, and to keep back part of the price of the land? Acts 5:3.

He can influence our dream state.

12: Now a thing was secretly brought to me, and mine ear received a little thereof.

13: In thoughts from the visions of the night, when deep sleep falleth on men,

14: Fear came upon me, and trembling, which made all my bones to shake.

15: Then a spirit passed before my face; the hair of my flesh stood up:

16: It stood still, but I could not discern the form thereof: an image was before mine eyes, there was silence, and I heard a voice, saying,

17: Shall mortal man be more just than God? shall a man be more pure than his maker? Job 4: 12-17.

He can cause fear.

For God hath not given us the spirit of fear; 1 Tim 1:7.

He can, at times, cause problems with our health.

So went Satan forth from the presence of the LORD, and smote Job with sore boils from the sole of his foot unto his crown. Job 2:7.

And ought not this woman, being a daughter of Abraham, whom Satan hath bound, lo, these eighteen years, be loosed from this bond on the sabbath day? Luke 13:16.

At times the enemy can engineer accidents.

Lord, have mercy on my son: for he is lunatick, and sore vexed: for ofttimes he falleth into the fire, and oft into the water. Matt. 17:15.

Lucifer sometimes brings people into our lives that are meant to hinder us.

22: Then Peter took him, and began to rebuke him, saying, Be it far from thee, Lord: this shall not be unto thee.

23: But he turned, and said unto Peter, Get thee behind me, Satan: thou art an offence unto me: for thou savourest not the things that be of God, but those that be of men. Matt. 16:23.

Satan is known as the prince of the power of the air,

Wherein in time past ye walked according to the course of this world, according to the prince of the power of the air, the spirit that now worketh in the children of disobedience: Eph. 2:2.

The devil is associated with darkness,

To open their eyes, and to turn them from darkness to light, and from the power of Satan unto God, that they may receive forgiveness of sins, and inheritance among them which are sanctified by faith that is in me. Acts 26:18.

He cannot ever separate us from our Supreme Commander.

38: For I am persuaded, that neither death, nor life, nor angels, nor principalities, nor powers, nor things present, nor things to come,

39: Nor height, nor depth, nor any other creature, shall be able to separate us from the love of God, which is in Christ Jesus our Lord. Romans 8: 38&39.

Know thy self

We have already gone over what you are as a Christian. A saint. A child of God. A heir. A friend of God. An elected representative of our Supreme Commander. We have discussed the gifts that are yours and the responsibilities that are yours also. Now we need to discuss the "fruits of the spirit." Those attributes that make you different from the others in this world. Fortunately Paul covers this in First Corinthians chapter 13.

1: Though I speak with the tongues of men and of angels, and have not charity, (love) I am become as sounding brass, or a tinkling cymbal.

2: And though I have the gift of prophecy, and understand all mysteries, and all knowledge; and though I have all faith, so that I could remove mountains, and have not charity, I am nothing. (Without love I am useless.)

3: And though I bestow all my goods to feed the poor, and though I give my body to be burned, and have not charity, it profiteth me nothing. (Without love nothing I do will matter.)

4: Charity suffereth long, and is kind; charity envieth not; charity vaunteth not itself, is not puffed up, (Love is in the act of waiting, is tender and considerate. Love wants the best for everyone. Love does not advertise itself nor is done for someone else's sake.)

5: Doth not behave itself unseemly, seeketh not her own, is not easily provoked, thinketh no evil; (Love is pure and is given equally to all. Love means one is not easily made angry. Love does not concern itself with evil.)

6: Rejoiceth not in iniquity, but rejoiceth in the truth; (Love does not involve itself with injustice or immoral behavior. Love loves the truth.)

7: Beareth all things, believeth all things, hopeth all things, endureth all things. (Love is the ability to endure through troubles. Love believes in goodness and hopes for only the best. Love has staying power.) 8: Charity never faileth: but whether there be prophecies, they shall fail; whether there be tongues, they shall cease; whether there be knowledge, it shall vanish away. (Love is forever.)

9: For we know in part, and we prophesy in part. (We can not see the whole picture.)

10: But when that which is perfect is come, then that which is in part shall be done away. (When Jesus returns then we shall know.)

11: When I was a child, I spake as a child, I understood as a child, I thought as a child: but when I became a man, I put away childish things. (To become a warrior of God we must digest the word in maturity).

12: For now we see through a glass, darkly; but then face to face: now I know in part; but then shall I know even as also I am known. (Like a fly on a Monet painting all we see is a blotch of paint. Our faith is all we have to know that in the end we will understand our part in the over all war.)

13: And now abideth faith, hope, charity, these three; but the greatest of these is charity. (Without Love we are nothing.)

Know thy God

Just who and what is God? How many thousands of books have been written on that subject? Books that are much more thorough then I could ever hope to be in this small volume. We'll just hit the highlights here. It will be up to you to study further. Let's start in Psalms. David had a very good idea just what were the attributes of God especially when it came to warfare.

God is our refuge and strength, a very present help in trouble. 46:1.

Behold, God is mine helper: the Lord is with them that uphold my soul. 54:4

So that a man shall say, Verily there is a reward for the righteous: verily he is a God that judgeth in the earth. 58:11

Because of his strength will I wait upon thee: for God is my defence. 59:9

In God is my salvation and my glory: the rock of my strength, and my refuge, is in God. 62:7

My flesh and my heart faileth: but God is the strength of my heart, and my portion for ever. 73:26

But God is the judge: he putteth down one, and setteth up another. 75:7

For the LORD God is a sun and shield: the LORD will give grace and glory: no good thing will he withhold from them that walk uprightly. 84:11

But the LORD is my defense; and my God is the rock of my refuge. 94:22

Here is Isaiah's description of the Supreme Commander,

2: For he shall grow up before him as a tender plant, and as a root out of a dry ground: he hath no form nor comeliness; and when we shall see him, there is no beauty that we should desire him.

3: He is despised and rejected of men; a man of sorrows, and acquainted with grief: and we hid as it were our faces from him; he was despised, and we esteemed him not. Isa. 53:2&3.

Hardly seems like the same person that we have all seen depicted in paintings. The apostles had to wait until the Transfiguration before seeing Jesus as He truly is,

And was transfigured before them: and his face did shine as the sun, and his raiment was white as the light. Matt. 17:2.

The Names of God

The battle manual lists several names for God:

13: And Moses said unto God, Behold, when I come unto the children of Israel, and shall say unto them, The God of your fathers hath sent me unto you; and they shall say to me, What is his name? what shall I say unto them?

14: And God said unto Moses, I AM THAT I AM: and he said, Thus shalt thou say unto the children of Israel, I AM hath sent me unto you. 15: And God said moreover unto Moses, Thus shalt thou say unto the children of Israel, The LORD God of your fathers, the God of Abraham, the God of Isaac, and the God of Jacob, hath sent me unto you: this is my name for ever, and this is my memorial unto all generations. Exodus 3: 13-15.

How many words could be written just to get to the bottom of the majesty of this statement? "I". Just one. The only. A singular unit, not two or more but the first and last. "Am" The quality of being. Having existence, to be. The only living God in the universe. The creator of all things.

More over He is the God of our fathers. The God of Abraham. The God of Isaac. The God of Jacob.

I am Alpha and Omega, the beginning and the ending, saith the Lord, which is, and which was, and which is to come, the Almighty. Rev. 1:8.

He created the universe, including the earth and man. He was here before the beginning of time and will be here after time ceases to exist. This notion is so important that it is repeated in Revelations 1:11, 21:16 and 22:13.

For unto us a child is born, unto us a son is given: and the government shall be upon his shoulder: and his name shall be called Wonderful, Counseller, The mighty God, The everlasting Father, The Prince of Peace. Isa. 9:6.

Wonderful, amazement and admiration for an entity so far above us combined with the realization of just what He has accomplished for us.

Counceller, ever present with encouragement and standing before the Father in our defense.

. The mighty God, defender of the elect.

The everlasting Father, Alpha and Omega. The first and last.

Prince of Peace, that peace that is more than the human mind can fathom.

Behold, a virgin shall be with child, and shall bring forth a son, and they shall call his name Emmanuel, which being interpreted is, God with us. Matt 1:23.

God with us, what a beautiful statement. The veil has been eliminated. All we have to do is say the word and we are in the presence of God Almighty. Praise His holy name!

He is our Rock.

And did all drink the same spiritual drink: for they drank of that spiritual Rock that followed them: and that Rock was Christ. 1 Cor 10:4.

More to the point of spiritual warfare this Rock is,

The LORD is my rock, and my fortress, and my deliverer; my God, my strength, in whom I will trust; my buckler, and the horn of my salvation, and my high tower. Psalms 18:2.

He is the foundation that all our duties rest upon. The instigator and provider.

HE IS JESUS CHRIST!

ADVANCED TRAINING
Part One

Tools

I was washing the dishes the other day and I happened to notice that all my table knives were bent on the end. It occurred to me that the reason they were bent is that they had all been used, at one time or another, as screwdrivers. The wrong tool for the wrong purpose. Some of the basic tools that we use for this spiritual war have already been discussed. There are others that should be covered.

Power

The first thing we are going to discuss in advanced training is just where does our power come from.

For the preaching of the cross is to them that perish foolishness; but unto us which are saved it is the power of God. 1 Cor. 1:18.

And God hath both raised up the Lord, and will also raise up us by his own power. 1 Cor 6:14

So we are now well aware that any power we have comes from God. There is no power in us that isn't regulated by the Holy Spirit.

We are "kept" by this power,

Who are kept by the power of God through faith unto salvation ready to be revealed in the last time. 1 Pet. 1:5.

This is a commitment by the Supreme Commander for our undertaking of spiritual warfare. He will provide the accommodations and support. He will specify the condition of our position and activity. He will provide for our necessities. He will honor and fulfill this commitment to us. He will guard, protect and defend His children. If we will only let Him.

For the kingdom of God is not in word, but in power. 1 Cor. 4:20.

Remember, child of God, it is not in others' outward appearance but in their deeds where we experience the power of the kingdom.

For though he was crucified through weakness, yet he liveth by the power of God. For we also are weak in him, but we shall live with him by the power of God toward you. 2 Cor 13:4.

My Jesus lives! It is the power of my God that accomplishes the fact that I, too, shall live.

And Jesus answering said unto them, Do ye not therefore err, because ye know not the scriptures, neither the power of God? Mark 12:24.

Again the battle manual is the written word of the power of God.

Truth

Withhold not thou thy tender mercies from me, O LORD: let thy lovingkindness and thy truth continually preserve me. Psalms 40:11.

To those of you who are experienced in spiritual warfare this comes at no surprise, THE TRUTH WILL PRESERVE YOU! It is quite easy to get wrapped up in religious rules and the cares of this temporary duty to the point that the basic truth is lost. Remember, dear child of God,

For the law was given by Moses, but grace and truth came by Jesus Christ. John 1:17.

WE ARE NOT UNDER LAW BUT GRACE!

In John 18:38 Pilate asked, " What is truth?" How very sad that a man of worldly power should ask such a question. Here are some answers, Pilate, you should have known.

All the paths of the LORD are mercy and truth unto such as keep his covenant and his testimonies.

Psalms 25:10.

For the word of the LORD is right; and all his works are done in truth. Psalms 33:4.

The word of God is truth! It is established and it is the truth forever.

The lip of truth shall be established for ever: but a lying tongue is but for a moment. Pro.12:19.

Also, in Proverbs are instructions for the spiritual warrior in regards to truth.

Buy the truth, and sell it not; also wisdom, and instruction, and understanding. Pro. 23:23.

Wisdom, instruction and understanding all demand the truth. The opposite of truth is, of course, a lie,

If we say that we have no sin, we deceive ourselves, and the truth is not in us.1 John 1:8

He that saith, I know him, and keepeth not his commandments, is a liar, and the truth is not in him.

1 John 2:4.

Rules of Engagement

2 COR. 6

3: Giving no offence in any thing, that the ministry be not blamed:

4: But in all things approving ourselves as the ministers of God, in much patience, in afflictions, in necessities, in distresses,

5: In stripes, in imprisonments, in tumults, in labours, in watchings, in fastings;

6: By pureness, by knowledge, by longsuffering, by kindness, by the Holy Ghost, by love unfeigned,

7: By the word of truth, by the power of God, by the armour of righteousness on the right hand and on the left,

8: By honour and dishonour, by evil report and good report: as deceivers, and yet true;

9: As unknown, and yet well known; as dying, and, behold, we live; as chastened, and not killed;

10: As sorrowful, yet alway rejoicing; as poor, yet making many rich; as having nothing, and yet possessing all things. 2 Cor. 6: 3-10.

These then are the rules of engagement for our battle to spread the truth of the Supreme Commander. One final thought, spiritual warriors,

Lead me in thy truth, and teach me: for thou art the God of my salvation; on thee do I wait all the day.

Psalms 25:5.

Weapons

Weapons can mean an item used in fighting or a means of persuading or arguing. We have already gone over the Full Armour of God but there are still others that need to be gone over,

The LORD hath opened his armoury, and hath brought forth the weapons of his indignation: Jer. 50:25.

They come from a far country, from the end of heaven, even the LORD, and the weapons of his indignation, Isa. 13:5.

What, exactly, are these weapons of God's indignation? His feeling of righteous anger toward His enemies? His annoyance provoked by unfair treatment? First off let's define what causes the anger of God.

And God's anger was kindled because he went: and the angel of the LORD stood in the way for an adversary against him. Now he was riding upon his ass, and his two servants were with him. Numbers 22:22.

This is the story of Balaam and it would be a good idea for the spiritual warrior to read the whole story but for now we find that God's indignation is with those that will not obey.

But unto them that are contentious, and do not obey the truth, but obey unrighteousness, indignation and wrath, Romans 2:18.

Here's what Paul had to say about these weapons to the church of Corinth,

3: For though we walk in the flesh, we do not war after the flesh:

4: (For the weapons of our warfare are not carnal, but mighty through God to the pulling down of strong holds;)

5: Casting down imaginations, and every high thing that exalteth itself against the knowledge of God, and bringing into captivity every thought to the obedience of Christ;

6: And having in a readiness to revenge all disobedience, when your obedience is fulfilled. 2 Cor 10:3-6

These weapons are not worldly. What good would earthly weapons do against a spiritual adversary?

To use these weapons there is a catch, your own obedience needs to be unquestioned.

For as by one man's disobedience many were made sinners, so by the obedience of one shall many be made righteous. Romans 5:19.

This then is the weapon of God's indignation, YOUR OBEDIENCE TO KEEP HIS COMMANDMENTS! Fellow warriors read the battle manual and follow those commandments for these weapons are mighty.

Mediation

Meditation is expressing your considered thoughts on a subject. It seems meditation has become problematic in the main line churches of our day. For some reason it has been equated with spiritualism, martial arts and yoga. Like I've said before I'm not interested in the precepts of various churches I am interested in the precepts of the Supreme Commander and here is what He had to say through Timothy,

13: Till I come, give attendance to reading, to exhortation, to doctrine.

14: Neglect not the gift that is in thee, which was given thee by prophecy, with the laying on of the hands of the presbytery.

15: Meditate upon these things; give thyself wholly to them; that thy profiting may appear to all.

16: Take heed unto thyself, and unto the doctrine; continue in them: for in doing this thou shalt both save thyself, and them that hear thee. 1 Timothy 4: 13-16.

We are told to meditate on reading, exhortation and doctrine. Reading the battle manual and listening to the Spirit as to its meaning for you. Exhortation means to strongly encourage or urge someone to do something. This is vitally important to the spiritual warrior. Listen to the Spirit. If He is directing you to do something…DO IT!.

Recently at a Bible study I was directed by the Spirit to lay hands on one of the guys there. He is going through a tremendous spiritual fight and after encouraging him with the word I had a sudden urge to lay my hands on the top of his head and on his back below the neck. I have had enough experience not to ignore these "urges". This is how the Spirit works. Act on those urges fellow warriors.

There was no one more concerned with meditation than the

Psalmist.

What to meditate about

Psalms 1:

1: Blessed is the man that walketh not in the counsel of the ungodly, nor standeth in the way of sinners, nor sitteth in the seat of the scornful.

2: But his delight is in the law of the LORD; and in his law doth he meditate day and night.

Psalms 77:

12: I will meditate also of all thy work, and talk of thy doings.

Psalms 119:

15: I will meditate in thy precepts, and have respect unto thy ways.

Psalms 119:

23: Princes also did sit and speak against me: but thy servant did meditate in thy statutes.

Psalms 119:

48: My hands also will I lift up unto thy commandments, which I have loved; and I will meditate in thy statutes.

Psalm 119:

78: Let the proud be ashamed; for they dealt perversely with me without a cause: but I will meditate in thy precepts.

Psalms 143:

5: I remember the days of old; I meditate on all thy works; I muse on the work of thy hands.

When to meditate

Psalms 63:

6: When I remember thee upon my bed, and meditate on thee in the night watches.

Psalms 119:

148: Mine eyes prevent the night watches, that I might meditate in thy word.

I think it is abundantly clear that this mediation is something that the spiritual warrior should think about doing.

ADVANCED TRAINING
Part Two

Support Groups

We have already gone, at length, into the Holy Ghost who is our main support but there are others such as,
Angels
And saith unto him, If thou be the Son of God, cast thyself down: for it is written, He shall give his angels charge concerning thee: and in their hands they shall bear thee up, lest at any time thou dash thy foot against a stone. Matt. 4:6

Thou madest him a little lower than the angels; thou crownedst him with glory and honour, and didst set him over the works of thy hands: Heb.2:7

For it is written, He shall give his angels charge over thee, to keep thee: Luke 4:10.

I have had a few encounters with angels and each time I stand amazed. The first time, as I recall, I was dumping some refuse at a local dump there was another fellow doing the same as I drove up. I went about my business and jumped back into my car and was about to leave when the guy motioned at me and walked over. I rolled down my window and the fella said, " You have to be careful. There is a divorce in your future if you don't change." Then he turned away and I sat stunned. I was a little discomforted by what he said(read scared) so I drove away. Back out on the street. I drove a short way before summoning up the courage to go back and see what the stranger meant. When I got back to the dump he was no longer there. Now, friends, I hadn't gone far enough down the road to lose sight of the driveway to that dump. There was no other exit. The man and his 3/4 ton truck had vanished.

Then the devil leaveth him, and, behold, angels came and ministered unto him. Matt. 4:11.

Another time that is vivid in my memory I and my mother were getting ready to go to town when there came a knock at the door. I opened it and a stranger who seemed to be distracted and perhaps unbalanced was standing there. "Could I get something to eat?" he asked. I was pretty skeptical of the guy and started making excuses on why I couldn't help him when I heard my mom call from the kitchen, "Who is it dear?" I explained the situation to her and said I was going to run him off but being a watchful provider of the grace of God my mom started fixing the man a sandwich.

I was uncomfortable with him coming into the house and watched closely as he ate. When he had finished, he said, " Thank you, brother." and waked back down our driveway to the road. I was suddenly overwhelmed with concern for the guy and went back into the house to call the police. The gal on the other end of the line remarked that an officer was in the immediate area and would look for the guy. I walked down to the roadway and saw the man still standing by the side of the road. I watched as a police cruiser slowly made his way toward us and watched incredulously as he passed us by. I watched for a few minutes thinking that the cruiser would turn around. It never did. I marched back up to the house and dialed 911. The gal on the other end told me that the officer had just called in and said that he had seen me but no one else although I was standing less that 100 yards from the guy.

Be not forgetful to entertain strangers: for thereby some have entertained angels unawares. Heb. 13:2.

A third instance occurred on September 14 1993. My son had been in a horrific auto accident and I was in a hospital waiting room with my family after thirty-six hours of prayer and the laying on of hands. (More on the gift of healing in another chapter.) The doctor I had first seen had told me that there was very little hope for my son and that he didn't expect him to make it through the night.

He had suffered a significant head injury and my wife and I found ourselves living a nightmare. Our whole world was focused on the pressure gauge attached to his skull. Our hearts would soar with each decrease in pressure and our hopes would be dashed at each increase. For a day and a half we didn't leave his side until the immediate danger had passed. Only then would we leave for food and sleep.

For some reason I wasn't hungry and as the others sat in the waiting room trying to decide where they would eat I fell into a deep sleep. I can't remember how long I slept but in that drowsy half awake state that one finds himself in when about to wake I felt a tap on my shoulder and a soft voice said, " Do not fear. He's going to be all right." My eyes snapped open only to see a vacant waiting room.

We took the boy home on January 3 1994 after the doctors had taught him to swallow, talk and walk all over again. Thank you, my Father.

Fellow Warriors

Not for that we have dominion over your faith, but are helpers of your joy: for by faith ye stand. 2 Cor. 1:24.

We have talked before about the need to be in a contingency of other spiritual warriors but we need to expand on the thought.

The Body of Christ

The Body of Christ is where the Supreme Commander lives. It is where He does His work. Everyone has a part, or more specifically, a job. We have already covered just what those jobs are now we will go into a bit more depth on how they relate to the spiritual warrior.

12: For as the body is one, and hath many members, and all the members of that one body, being many, are one body: so also is Christ.

13: For by one Spirit are we all baptized into one body, whether we be Jews or Gentiles, whether we be bond or free; and have been all made to drink into one Spirit.

14: For the body is not one member, but many. 1 Cor. 12:12-14. God does not give these jobs for our own benefit but to be used for the instruction and improvement of those that we have been instructed to serve. Again, it is only through God's power that these "gifts" can be used effectively. We are to combine with other spiritual warriors, with other gifts and support each other,

16: The cup of blessing which we bless, is it not the communion of the blood of Christ? The bread which we break, is it not the communion of the body of Christ?

17: For we being many are one bread, and one body: for we are all partakers of that one bread.

1 Cor. 10:16&17.

When in combination with other saints we support each other for improvement and learning,

For the perfecting of the saints, for the work of the ministry, for the edifying of the body of Christ:

Eph. 4:12.

All who are spiritual warriors are born of the Spirit(The Holy Ghost) and are members of this Body of Christ. We have been given gifts that correspond and interweave with others in the Body. This Body functions best when all of its members use their infinite varieties of skills and talents, their natural abilities and inclinations to educate and improve each other. This is God's plan for His church.

Spiritual Freedom

Spiritual freedom is necessary for the Body of Christ to function. The success of America in its early days was based on this freedom. The laws and policies of early America gave the Body the much needed cooperation to flourish and operate. In those days there was no centralized authority to govern the workings of the Body of Christ. The separation of church and state had not been enacted, indeed, was never envisioned either by the church or the government.

Slowly, like Job's leviathan, the government of the U.S. began to centralize after the War Between the States. When the depression of the nineteen thirties hit, this centralization solidified in ways that were to become disastrous for the country and the working of the Body of Christ. Since the reason for the economic disaster was laid on some type of lack of success of the free market system personal responsibility was replaced with a "nanny state". Individuals were no longer masters of their own fate but were now pawns influenced by an uncontrollable series of events. The United States began policies that destroyed the individual and any "can do" attitude that remained. Instead of all men are created equal we became a country of some are more equal than others. The Body of Christ was also affected by " professionals" who took over and also refused to value the individual.

I am reminded of a time in the late sixties. I was involved with the peace movement and one woman stands out in my memory. She was from the Kentucky woods and had that inherent common sense that seems to be pervasive in hill people. At the time she was in her eighties and of small stature but with a fierceness in her eyes. She had been arrested at a sit-in and I liked her enough to sit in on the court where her case was being tried. I will never forget when the judge asked, "How do you plead?" She raised herself up to her full 4 foot 9 inches and looked at the judge straight in the eyes as she replied," Judge, I will not plead. There's laws for us'ins and laws for you'uns and they are not the same."

That about said it all for the country as well as the church.

Happily, "the times they are a'changin." In the Body of Christ there is a revolution going on. There is a subculture of spiritual warriors who are rethinking the status quo. They have recognized that the U.S. has changed its nature. From the individualism of its people to the mob rule of Democracy and along with it the church. These warriors are in full rebellion. They have rejected the church of hired professionals. They have come to realize that the Body of Christ is not found in Doctor of Theology degrees and 2 hour business meetings. Our "battle cry" is that the church of God should be controlled by the Holy Spirit who has handed out gifts to each of its members, to be used by them for the spiritual war that we find ourselves in.

Here is the truth, fellow warriors. THERE ARE NO MEMBERS OF THE BODY OF CHRIST WHO HAVE LITTLE OR NO IMPORTANCE OR VALUE! Each member has been ordained with specialized gifts that are needed by the whole.

The Supreme Commander has endowed His body with individuals who are vital to it's over all health. Thus the body is balanced with authority given by the Holy Spirit to proclaim the truth.

ADVANCED TRAINING
Part Three

Logistics

Logistics basically means how to handle the details of an operation. The first two details we are going to look at are the differences between our needs and what we desire. Take into consideration that the philosopher Descarte once remarked that, "desire is the beginning of all sorrows."

30: But their scribes and Pharisees murmured against his disciples, saying, Why do ye eat and drink with publicans and sinners?

31: And Jesus answering said unto them, They that are whole need not a physician; but they that are sick.

32: I came not to call the righteous, but sinners to repentance. Luke 5: 30-32.

I have spent a great deal of time in various churches. Baptist to Pentecostal. Methodist to Catholic.

The problem with them all is that they are full of Christians. We cannot "preach to the choir" and expect to reach the people who need the gospel the most. Our Supreme Commander leads from the front, explaining to us that it is not the healthy who need a doctor. At some time in this spiritual battle you will have to leave the safe confines of the church and advance on the enemy.

27: Consider the lilies how they grow: they toil not, they spin not; and yet I say unto you, that Solomon in all his glory was not arrayed like one of these.

28: If then God so clothe the grass, which is to day in the field, and to morrow is cast into the oven; how much more will he clothe you, O ye of little faith?

29: And seek not ye what ye shall eat, or what ye shall drink, neither be ye of doubtful mind.

30: For all these things do the nations of the world seek after: and your Father knoweth that ye have need of these things.

31: But rather seek ye the kingdom of God; and all these things shall be added unto you.

Here's your answer to all those Word of Faith adherents. Our Father knows our needs before we even ask for them. When desires begin to out weigh needs is when the warrior finds himself in trouble. So what does the Supreme Commander say? Seek ye the kingdom of God. Well what is this kingdom of God and how do we seek it?

Just what is this Kingdom of God?

For the kingdom of God is not meat and drink; but righteousness, and peace, and joy in the Holy Ghost.

Romans 14:17.

A kingdom is a domain ruled by a king. Our king is none other that Almighty God. He is our head of state.

Who Owns the Kingdom?

And he lifted up his eyes on his disciples, and said, Blessed be ye poor: for yours is the kingdom of God. Luke 6:20.

The Supreme Commander had a lot to say about the treatment of the poor and that makes a great study on it's own. Suffice it to say, the poor own the kingdom so as a class it is important to remember our singular duty to them.

Where is the Kingdom?

Neither shall they say, Lo here! or, lo there! for, behold, the kingdom of God is within you. Luke 17:21.

He's talking to you, warrior. There's no use looking around for the kingdom. It is right where He left it. Inside of you.

Who makes up this Kingdom?

16: But Jesus called them unto him, and said, Suffer little children to come unto me, and forbid them not: for of such is the kingdom of God.

17: Verily I say unto you, Whosoever shall not receive the kingdom of God as a little child shall in no wise enter therein. Luke 18: 16&17.

Who will have a hard time entering into the Kingdom?

And when Jesus saw that he was very sorrowful, he said, How hardly shall they that have riches enter into the kingdom of God! Luke 18:24.

Perhaps the single most "need" reveling chapter in the Bible is the 23rd Psalm.

1: The LORD is my shepherd (one who gives spiritual guidance and care); I shall not want (lack or be short of something desirable or essential).

The trick here, child of God, is to know the difference between what is a selfish desire and what is essential.

2: He maketh me to lie down in green pastures: he leadeth me beside the still waters.

God does give us the peace that passes all understanding...if we will just let Him.

3: He restoreth my soul: he leadeth me in the paths of righteousness for his name's sake.

The Holy Spirit will repair and return our soul to where it was when we first understood the Gospel. We can be reinstated as long as we are willing to listen.

4: Yea, though I walk through the valley of the shadow of death, I will fear no evil: for thou art with me; thy rod and thy staff they comfort me.

The rod is the rod of correction and the staff is the staff of direction. He will show the way.

5: Thou preparest a table before me in the presence of mine enemies: thou anointest my head with oil; my cup runneth over.

God will show us how to resist Satan and no longer fear him. The Supreme Commander has already forgiven the elect. What else could we need?

6: Surely goodness and mercy shall follow me all the days of my life: and I will dwell in the house of the LORD for ever, Amen.

Remember, recruit, GOD IS GOOD! He is motivated by compassion and forgiveness. No bad thing comes from God.

ADVANCED TRAINING
Part Four

Listening to God

If there is anything that I have been teaching here it is the importance of listening to God. How can we hear if we are not listening? Listening is something that is applied to advice and a request. It requires effort. It means paying attention to someone. In this case, God. What could be more important to the warrior than listening to the words of his Supreme Commander? The only thing more important is actually hearing. There is a difference, fellow believer, hearing implies that we are listening to evidence.

Listen, O isles, unto me; and hearken, ye people, from far; The LORD hath called me from the womb; from the bowels of my mother hath he made mention of my name. Isa. 49:1.

Too long for most of us (myself included) we have heard the words but have not understood. Yes we are elected from the beginning of time but our free-will is this: Are we willing to let the Holy Ghost work through us? Are we willing to give up ourselves and do what He has commanded?

Here is my own confession. When I was about twenty years of age I fell into a deep sleep and dreamed. The Holy Ghost spoke to me through this dream. This dream is the only one I have ever remembered and it took place almost 35 years ago. In the dream I found myself on a bus. The bus was filled with people from scripture. I saw Ruth and Naomi still together after all this time. I saw Jacob and all of his sons seated and talking. I saw the four, Matthew, Mark, Luke and John still writing in notebooks after all the years. I saw Paul jotting down notes on a pad. I saw John the Baptist still dressed in rags but his face still shining. Next to him was seated my Jesus. His whole being pulsing with glory and love. As I boarded the bus they all looked up and smiled. My Lord then said something that shook me to my foundations. " Write a book for me Steven." That was all He said but it bored into my mind and soul. Like I said that was thirty-five years ago but the dream is still fresh in my mind. Please, my fellow believers, don't let so much time pass before doing what you are told.

Understanding God

27: Make me to understand the way of thy precepts: so shall I talk of thy wondrous works. 34: Give me understanding, and I shall keep thy law; yea, I shall observe it with my whole heart. Psalms 119: 27&34.

The reason that we, as spiritual warriors, often have problems in understanding the Supreme Commander is that we try to understand with our own mental capacities. Every one of us sees the world differently through our own preconceived notions based on our experiences. I can read a verse in the battle manual and come up with a completely different way of analyzing and interpretating what that verse means than you will. The Supreme Commander aims for us to understand His word. The battle manual is there for the sole purpose of training us to be effective warriors. The thing is that we need God's help even with this,

Trust in the LORD with all thine heart; and lean not unto thine own understanding. Prov. 3:5.

Moreover I advise you, fellow warriors, that no matter how sincere someone seems, how logically their arguments seem, how intelligent their answers are do not accept everything that you hear until you have asked the Supreme Commander Himself. INCLUDING THE WORDS FOUND HERE! THERE IS NO HUMAN WHO IS INFALLIBLE. There is only one who is infallible and that personage is God. TRUST ONLY HIM!

But the anointing which ye have received of him abideth in you, and ye need not that any man teach you: but as the same anointing teacheth you of all things, and is truth, and is no lie, and even as it hath taught you, ye shall abide in him. 1 John 2:27.

Waiting

Waiting on the Lord is not like the church's, shut up, sit down and listen. Waiting on the Lord is active.

5: I wait for the LORD, my soul doth wait, and in his word do I hope.

6: My soul waiteth for the Lord more than they that watch for the morning: I say, more than they that watch for the morning. Psalms 130:5&6.

How can you wait more? Fellow warrior test everything on what the battle manual says. Then wait more for the word to be made plain through the Holy Ghost.

Lead me in thy truth, and teach me: for thou art the God of my salvation; on thee do I wait all the day.

Psalm 25:5.

While you are waiting and listening the Supreme Commander will be teaching you. We need to allow Him to speak to us. This is just another way of dying to self.

Rest in the LORD, and wait patiently for him: fret not thyself because of him who prospereth in his way, because of the man who bringeth wicked devices to pass. Psalms 37:7.

Wait on the LORD, and keep his way, and he shall exalt thee to inherit the land: when the wicked are cut off, thou shalt see it. Psalms 37:34.

Follow the Supreme Commander's commandments. He is faithful and just. He will see you through.

And now, Lord, what wait I for? my hope is in thee. Psalms 39:7.

Read Proverbs 8:

1: Doth not wisdom cry? and understanding put forth her voice?

2: She standeth in the top of high places, by the way in the places of the paths.

3: She crieth at the gates, at the entry of the city, at the coming in at the doors.

4: Unto you, O men, I call; and my voice is to the sons of man.

5: O ye simple, understand wisdom: and, ye fools, be ye of an understanding heart.

6: Hear; for I will speak of excellent things; and the opening of my lips shall be right things.

7: For my mouth shall speak truth; and wickedness is an abomination to my lips.

8: All the words of my mouth are in righteousness; there is nothing froward or perverse in them.

9: They are all plain to him that understandeth, and right to them that find knowledge.

10: Receive my instruction, and not silver; and knowledge rather than choice gold.

11: For wisdom is better than rubies; and all the things that may be desired are not to be compared to it.

12: I wisdom dwell with prudence, and find out knowledge of witty inventions. 13: The fear of the LORD is to hate evil: pride, and arrogancy, and the evil way, and the froward mouth, do I hate.

14: Counsel is mine, and sound wisdom: I am understanding; I have strength.

15: By me kings reign, and princes decree justice.

16: By me princes rule, and nobles, even all the judges of the earth.

17: I love them that love me; and those that seek me early shall find me.

18: Riches and honour are with me; yea, durable riches and righteousness.

19: My fruit is better than gold, yea, than fine gold; and my revenue than choice silver.

20: I lead in the way of righteousness, in the midst of the paths of judgment:

21: That I may cause those that love me to inherit substance; and I will fill their treasures.

22: The LORD possessed me in the beginning of his way, before his works of old.

23: I was set up from everlasting, from the beginning, or ever the earth was.

24: When there were no depths, I was brought forth; when there were no fountains abounding with water.

25: Before the mountains were settled, before the hills was I brought forth:

26: While as yet he had not made the earth, nor the fields, nor the highest part of the dust of the world.

27: When he prepared the heavens, I was there: when he set a compass upon the face of the depth:

28: When he established the clouds above: when he strengthened the fountains of the deep:

29: When he gave to the sea his decree, that the waters should not pass his commandment: when he appointed the foundations of the earth:

30: Then I was by him, as one brought up with him: and I was daily his delight, rejoicing always before him;

31: Rejoicing in the habitable part of his earth; and my delights were with the sons of men.

32: Now therefore hearken unto me, O ye children: for blessed are they that keep my ways.

33: Hear instruction, and be wise, and refuse it not.

34: Blessed is the man that heareth me, watching daily at my gates, waiting at the posts of my doors.

35: For whoso findeth me findeth life, and shall obtain favour of the LORD.

36: But he that sinneth against me wrongeth his own soul: all they that hate me love death.

ADVANCED TRAINING
Part Five

Judging

One of the most misunderstood subjects found in the battle manual is the subject of judging. As we have already seen. On the one hand we are told,

Do ye not know that the saints shall judge the world? and if the world shall be judged by you, are ye unworthy to judge the smallest matters? 1 Cor 6:2.

On the other hand we find,

Judge not, that ye be not judged. Matt 7:1.
Is this a contradiction? I have said earlier that taken out of context a warrior can get the battle manual to say almost anything. So which is it? Are we to judge or not? Well first of all God makes a clear distinction between the elect and the unbeliever.

But I say unto you, That whosoever is angry with his brother without a cause shall be in danger of the judgment: and whosoever shall say to his brother, Raca, shall be in danger of the council: but whosoever shall say, Thou fool, shall be in danger of hell fire. Matt. 5:22.

Here the Supreme Commander is clearly talking about fellow believers. We must be very careful in the way we treat our fellow warriors. We are all in this together.

10: But why dost thou judge thy brother? or why dost thou set at nought thy brother? for we shall all stand before the judgment seat of Christ.

11: For it is written, As I live, saith the Lord, every knee shall bow to me, and every tongue shall confess to God.

12: So then every one of us shall give account of himself to God.

13: Let us not therefore judge one another any more: but judge this rather, that no man put a stumblingblock or an occasion to fall in his brother's way. Romans 14:10-13.

Speak not evil one of another, brethren. He that speaketh evil of his brother, and judgeth his brother, speaketh evil of the law, and judgeth the law: but if thou judge the law, thou art not a doer of the law, but a judge. James 4:11.

These verses make it perfectly clear that we should exercise caution when dealing with our fellow warriors but that doesn't mean that we do not judge. Jesus said,

Judge not according to the appearance, but judge righteous judgment. John 7:24.

Not only are we to judge the world but we are to ultimately judge the angels. We are to judge one another but we are not to be judged by unbelievers.

1: Dare any of you, having a matter against another, go to law before the unjust, and not before the saints?

2: Do ye not know that the saints shall judge the world? and if the world shall be judged by you, are ye unworthy to judge the smallest matters?

3: Know ye not that we shall judge angels? how much more things that pertain to this life?

4: If then ye have judgments of things pertaining to this life, set them to judge who are least esteemed in the church.

5: I speak to your shame. Is it so, that there is not a wise man among you? no, not one that shall be able to judge between his brethren?

6: But brother goeth to law with brother, and that before the unbelievers.1 Cor. 6:2-6.

Paul had no trouble judging even if he was not there physically,

For I verily, as absent in body, but present in spirit, have judged already, as though I were present, concerning him that hath so done this deed, 1 Cor. 5:3.

The thing about Paul was that he knew which side of the bread the butter was on. He realized that it was not he that judged but the Supreme Commander who judged through him,

3: But with me it is a very small thing that I should be judged of you, or of man's judgment: yea, I judge not mine own self.

4: For I know nothing by myself; yet am I not hereby justified: but he that judgeth me is the Lord.

5: Therefore judge nothing before the time, until the Lord come, who both will bring to light the hidden things of darkness, and will make manifest the counsels of the hearts: and then shall every man have praise of God. 1 Cor.4: 3-5.

Paul understood the nature of humans and knew,

For if we would judge ourselves, we should not be judged. 1 Cor. 11:31.

I think we have made a case that we are to judge. But how? We are not to judge eternally only God has that option. We are talking about His creation. Unless the person has rejected the Supreme Commander out of hand, we are not capable of discerning everything about an individual. Even a spiritual warrior is inept at understanding motives. We cannot weigh his actions. Nor can we perceive just what opportunities are involved in a given situation unless God reveals it to us.

Open thy mouth, judge righteously, and plead the cause of the poor and needy. Proverbs 31:9.

He judged the cause of the poor and needy; then it was well with him: was not this to know me? saith the LORD. Jer.22:16.

Ye shall do no unrighteousness in judgment: thou shalt not respect the person of the poor, nor honour the person of the mighty: but in righteousness shalt thou judge thy neighbour. Lev. 19:15.

Epilogue

It is my fervent hope that all of you who have read this book have gained an understanding of just what is entailed in being a spiritual warrior. Central to my thesis is that we cannot do it without a thorough understanding of the ground rules. I have strived, with the grace of the Supreme Commander, to list these tenets in a logical manner. Without Him I am nothing. You will notice a bit of repetition in this book. It is there for a reason. It is my belief that certain ideas or concepts need to be emblazoned on our mind so as to become second nature. I decided or perhaps it was decided for me to add a word, as promised, about virtue. Virtue has several meanings. Virtue can mean behavior that shows high moral standards. It can mean to have a good or desirable moral quality. In the case of spiritual warriors I like to think of the word in its Latin base of valor or courage in the face of danger. Spiritual warfare is not for the faint of heart.

3: According as his divine power hath given unto us all things that pertain unto life and godliness, through the knowledge of him that hath called us to glory and virtue:
4: Whereby are given unto us exceeding great and precious promises: that by these ye might be partakers of the divine nature, having escaped the corruption that is in the world through lust. 5: And beside this, giving all diligence, add to your faith virtue; and to virtue knowledge; 2 Peter 1:3-5.

To me faith is first and then valor. Spiritual warfare is fraught with danger in these latter days. Our Supreme Commander has given us His own power if we have the wisdom to use it. If we do, we are promised glory and virtue. Praise God!

And the whole multitude sought to touch him: for there went virtue out of him, and healed them all. Luke 6:19.

His courage healed them. His valor in coming to earth to save His children caused them to be healed immediately and for ever. Praise His holy name!

And Jesus said, Somebody hath touched me: for I perceive that virtue is gone out of me. Luke 8:46.

In the Greek virtue, here, means inherent power, power residing in a man by virtue of its nature.

When healing expect a feeling of loss, of exhaustion. Its part of the deal. God hardly ever repeals the laws of nature. For every action there is an equal reaction. Expect it ahead of time and you won't find it surprising. I have felt this loss and the tiredness that comes from a healing session. One can experience physical pain. A healing can bring with it distress, discomfort or disorder. Expect it.

What He's done for others He can do for you, my fellow warrior!

30: And Jesus, immediately knowing in himself that virtue had gone out of him, turned him about in the press, and said, Who touched my clothes?

31: And his disciples said unto him, Thou seest the multitude thronging thee, and sayest thou, Who touched me?

32: And he looked round about to see her that had done this thing.

33: But the woman fearing and trembling, knowing what was done in her, came and fell down before him, and told him all the truth.

34: And he said unto her, Daughter, thy faith hath made thee whole; go in peace, and be whole of thy plague. Mark 5:30-34.

We absolutely must give credit where credit is due. He is still in the healing business and so should we.

6: Be careful for nothing; but in every thing by prayer and supplication with thanksgiving let your requests be made known unto God.

7: And the peace of God, which passeth all understanding, shall keep your hearts and minds through Christ Jesus.

8: Finally, brethren, whatsoever things are true, whatsoever things are honest, whatsoever things are just, whatsoever things are pure, whatsoever things are lovely, whatsoever things are of good report; if there be any virtue, and if there be any praise, think on these things.

9: Those things, which ye have both learned, and received, and heard, and seen in me, do: and the God of peace shall be with you. Phil. 4:6-8.

Fellow warriors you should be doing the same things. This is the vitality of the gospel that we not only do the things that the Supreme Commander did but even more as the scriptures read.

Just recently one of my students came to me and said that her doctors had found a grapefruit size tumor on her liver. Needless to say she was scared to death. She asked if I might pray for her and lay hands on her. I immediately prayed and placed one hand on her back and one just to the front of where her liver would be. I could actually feel the tumor. It felt round and hard and totally unnatural. I continued to pray and visually "pump" what virtue I have through the ordinance of my Supreme Commander. Later I went to my own, personal, support group of warriors. Together we prayed for the woman. Fellow warriors, you can't do any better in this life than to be the witnesses to a handful of true warriors of God praying earnestly for someone they had never met. Praise God! Three days later the young woman came to me and said that a second MRI had found nothing. Nothing! Nothing! Nothing!

THERE IS NOTHING THAT IS IMPOSSIBLE TO THE CREATOR OF THE UNIVERSE IF WE ONLY OBEY HIS HOLY WORD! TO GOD BE THE GLORY.

The Seven Promises of God

I feel that I would be amiss if I didn't outline the promises of God to the valiant warrior. They are:

One

God promised that His warriors would never be tempted beyond their endurance. 1Cor.10:13.

In Jude 1:24,
Now unto him that is able to keep you from falling, and to present you faultless before the presence of his glory with exceeding joy,
Then the king commanded, and they brought Daniel, and cast him into the den of lions. Now the king spake and said unto Daniel, Thy God whom thou servest continually, he will deliver thee. Dan. 6:16.

Get this through your skull, recruits, you are under God's protection. There is NO FEAR!

Two

God has promised to supply every need. (Phil. 4:19.) Be aware that He said needs. He is not speaking of luxuries. Sorry about that warriors. Shelter, food, clothing, companionship, love and salvation. These are our needs. As a character on a favorite cartoon says, " Simplify, man, simplify."
On a trip to Mexico, years ago, a friend was amazed at the

poverty of the people. He was even more amazed when he entered the village church and saw the gold statues and rich tapestries that adorned the worship area. This thought went through his mind, " Why not sell these riches and at least supply the basic needs of the people?" Why indeed?

Three

His sufficient grace has been promised to His warriors. (2 Cor. 12:9). By this time you should have a basic understanding of this thing called grace. It is the warrior's way of standing before God almighty.
When the veil was torn at the death of Christ, a new era began. In the days before this, if one needed to speak to God, he needed an "intercessor." Someone to go before God for him. The priest or rabbi would be the one to go before God by entering the holy of holies passing through the veil to seek the Almighty. An interesting sidelight is that the priest had a cord tied around his ankle. This cord was to enable the other priests to pull out his corpse if the priest wasn't right with God. Quite a job, hey? When the veil was torn, it meant that from that time on we no longer needed a priest. Praise God! We have immediate and direct access, through grace, to the very Creator of the Universe!

Four

All things work together for the good of God's warriors is yet another promise,
And we know that all things work together for good to them that love God, to them who are the called according to his purpose. Romans 8:28.
Sometimes it can seem quite daunting to believe that all things work to the good but this is where the warrior's faith comes in. Faith

is the anchor that stops us from drifting when the enemy attacks. Be sure, fellow warriors, we are a protected species. The insurance of our faith is full. We have a contract with the Supreme Commander for protection from future loss. We are assured of reimbursement for losses in the present. The anchor holds.

Five

God has promised us victory over death. The end of our contest WILL be successful. The defeat of our opponent is assured. He who is the personification of death will be cast into a lake of fire never to trouble mankind again.

51: Behold, I shew you a mystery; We shall not all sleep, but we shall all be changed,

52: In a moment, in the twinkling of an eye, at the last trump: for the trumpet shall sound, and the dead shall be raised incorruptible, and we shall be changed.

53: For this corruptible must put on incorruption, and this mortal must put on immortality.

54: So when this corruptible shall have put on incorruption, and this mortal shall have put on immortality, then shall be brought to pass the saying that is written, Death is swallowed up in victory.

55: O death, where is thy sting? O grave, where is thy victory?

56: The sting of death is sin; and the strength of sin is the law.

57: But thanks be to God, which giveth us the victory through our Lord Jesus Christ.

58: Therefore, my beloved brethren, be ye stedfast, unmoveable, always abounding in the work of the Lord, forasmuch as ye know that your labour is not in vain in the Lord. 1 Cor. 15: 51-58.

Six

Another promise that God stated is that those that believe in my Jesus will be saved.

He that believeth and is baptized shall be saved; but he that believeth not shall be damned. Mark 16:16.

Then Peter said unto them, Repent, and be baptized every one of you in the name of Jesus Christ for the remission of sins, and ye shall receive the gift of the Holy Ghost. Acts 2:38.

Seven

Finally and most importantly God has promised this:

28: And I give unto them eternal life; and they shall never perish, neither shall any man pluck them out of my hand.

29: My Father, which gave them me, is greater than all; and no man is able to pluck them out of my Father's hand. John 10: 27&28.

There is one final promise that I want to cover separately. This promise is found in Romans, chapter eight, verse one. It reads,

There is therefore now no condemnation to them which are in Christ Jesus, who walk not after the flesh, but after the Spirit.

I remember the first time that this verse jumped off the page of my Bible and bored into my mind.

How incredibly excited I became as the full intent of the verse became clear. To this day just reading Paul's words through the inspiration of my Jesus thrill me anew.

No condemnation? No disapproval? The punishment must fit the crime but where there is no crime there is no punishment. How many times with the legalistic mumbo-jumbo of the church was I told the opposite. That I was a worm, a sinner and a reprobate. Then here is Paul officially declaring each one of us as fit for use by the Supreme

Commander. There would never again be a question of loss only of gain. My Jesus would never disapprove of me. He would never denounce me.

Then I read it again and realized that it said, There is therefore NOW, not some pie in the sky wait until you die promise but right NOW... TODAY! Not when we all get to heaven but NOW! I was raised like a lot of "church" folks to wait till someday but here it was in black and white NOW! Praise His holy name. If I walk with His Holy Spirit I don't have to wait to be "happy in Jesus." I can be happy NOW! Fellow warriors you can't be happy yesterday. It's dead and gone. You can't be happy tomorrow. It never gets here. Warriors you need to be happy today. From the precise moment you were elected to serve there was no condemnation. At this present time there is no condemnation. Under the present circumstances there is NO condemnation. As a consequence of the sacrifice of the Supreme Commander there is NO condemnation. Now and forever there is NO condemnation.

This book was intended for those that have embraced spiritual warfare and have decided to keep the commandments of our Supreme Commander. If you have stumbled onto this book but are not a believer I invite you right now to pray that God will make His word clear to you. Come join Him and us in the great commission. Give your heart, soul, mind and body to the Creator of the universe. Ask Him to change your heart and work through you to change the hearts of others. This is how the world can be changed. No other way.

In conclusion,

No weapon that is formed against thee shall prosper; and every tongue that shall rise against thee in judgment thou shalt condemn. This is the heritage of the servants of the LORD, and their righteousness is of me, saith the LORD. Isaiah 54:17

In other words, WE WIN!

In closing I offer this verse,

He which testifieth these things saith, Surely I come quickly. Amen. Even so, come, Lord Jesus. Rev. 22:20.

THE END

Printed in the United States
47784LVS00001BA/445